Digital Ethics in the Age of AI
Navigating the ethical frontier today and beyond

Digital Ethics in the Age of AI
Navigating the ethical frontier today and beyond

DR JULIE E. MEHAN

IT Governance Publishing

IT Governance Publishing Ltd
Unit 3, Clive Court
Bartholomew's Walk
Cambridgeshire Business Park
Ely, Cambridgeshire
CB7 4EA
United Kingdom
www.itgovernancepublishing.co.uk

First published in the United Kingdom in 2024 by IT Governance Publishing.

ISBN 978-1-78778-549-6

FOREWORD

In the ever-evolving landscape of technology and artificial intelligence (AI), 2023 marked a pivotal moment in our collective journey toward understanding and addressing the profound ethical questions raised by AI. As we stand at the intersection of innovation and ethics, this book serves as a guiding light as it attempts to illuminate the complex and dynamic terrain of AI and its ethical implications in a highly digitized world. Digital ethics, the study of moral principles that govern our digital interactions and AI-driven decision-making, has become a critical framework for navigating this transformative landscape.

AI has woven itself into the fabric of our daily lives, influencing how we work, communicate, and even perceive the world. Its transformative power is undeniable, yet it brings a host of ethical dilemmas that challenge our moral compass. From concerns surrounding bias and fairness to issues of privacy, accountability, and the potential for job displacement, AI ethics has emerged as a critical discourse that transcends the boundaries of technology and touches the core of our humanity.

In this era characterized by the remarkable growth of AI, there emerges a profound ethical dimension that demands our attention and introspection. This book presents a timely and significant addition to the ongoing discourse that explores the ethical implications of the transformative power of AI in general and the new and disruptive AI technologies, such as generative AI.

Its pages reflect a world where AI machines can create, compose, and imagine with astonishing creativity. From generating human-like text to crafting lifelike images and music, generative AI has broken the boundaries of what was once considered the exclusive domain of human creativity. But with these incredible capabilities come profound ethical questions.

In this book, we encounter the complex intersections between AI and ethics, where creativity, bias, privacy, and authenticity are intertwined. We are challenged to consider how AI influences our perception of reality, how it shapes our cultural and artistic landscapes, and how it can either perpetuate or mitigate societal biases.

But the book is intended to engage us in ongoing dialogs about the responsible development and use of AI. It challenges us to envision a future where the fruits of AI innovation are harnessed to benefit humanity while preserving our values and principles. It is in part a continuation of my first book on AI published in June 2022 and reflects many of the landmark changes that have occurred since that time. My first book on AI and ethics focused on the ethical concerns associated largely with the implementation of AI in various sectors of society and the economy. I would be remiss if I did not hark back to this and emphasize also the environmental impact of AI – another aspect of AI and ethics. While AI has many positive applications for the environment, there is also a negative side to the explosion of AI and its associated infrastructure. The ever-increasing number of data centers that house AI servers produce significant electronic waste. They are large consumers of water, which is becoming scarce in many places. They rely on critical minerals and rare elements, which are often mined unsustainably. And they use massive amounts of electricity, spurring the emission of planet-warming greenhouse gases.

Foreword

As we embark on this exploration of AI and ethics, let us remember that the future of AI is not predetermined. It is shaped by our choices, our ethics, and our commitment to a world where technology enhances our lives while respecting our shared humanity.

I hope to provide an indispensable guide for anyone who wishes to navigate this ever-evolving landscape thoughtfully and ethically.

ABOUT THE AUTHOR

Dr Julie Mehan is semi-retired, but still serves as a Professor at the University of Maryland Global College (UMGC), where she teaches Digital Ethics, Cyberterrorism, and Information Systems in Organizations. It was the students in her digital ethics and computer science classes who inspired this book.

Until her semi-retirement to the wonderful state of Florida, she was the Founder and President of JEMStone Strategies and a principal in a strategic consulting firm in the state of Virginia.

Dr Mehan has been a career Government Service employee, a strategic consultant, and an entrepreneur – which either demonstrates her flexibility or inability to hold on to a steady job! She has led business operations, as well as IT governance and cybersecurity-related services, including designing and leading white and blackhat penetration exercises, certification and accreditation, systems security engineering process improvement, and cybersecurity strategic planning and program management. During her professional years, she delivered cybersecurity and related privacy services to senior Department of Defense, Federal Government, and commercial clients working in Italy, Australia, Canada, Belgium, Germany, and the US.

She has served on the President's Partnership for Critical Infrastructure Security, Task Force on Interdependency and Vulnerability Assessments. Dr Mehan was chair for the development of criteria for the Information Systems Security Engineering Professional (ISSEP) certification, a voting board member for development of the International Systems

Security Professional Certification Scheme (ISSPCS), and Chair of the Systems Certification Working Group of the International Systems Security Engineering Association.

Dr Mehan graduated *summa cum laude* with a PhD from Capella University, with dual majors in Information Technology Management and Organizational Psychology. Her research was focused on success and failure criteria for Chief Information Security Officers (CISOs) in large government and commercial organizations and development of a dynamic model of Chief Security Officer (CSO) leadership. She holds an MA with honors in International Relations Strategy and Law from Boston University, and a BS in History and Languages from the University of New York.

Dr Mehan was elected 2003 Woman of Distinction by the Women of Greater Washington. She has published numerous articles including "Framework for Reasoning About Security – A Comparison of the Concepts of Immunology and Security"; "System Dynamics, Criminal Behavior Theory and Computer-Enabled Crime"; "The Value of Information-Based Warfare to Affect Adversary Decision Cycles"; and "Information Operations in Kosovo: Mistakes, Missteps, and Missed Opportunities", released in Cyberwar 4.0.

Dr Mehan is the author of several books published by ITGP: *Artificial Intelligence*, published in 2020 and revised in 2023; *Insider Threat*, published in 2016; *CyberWar, CyberTerror, CyberCrime and CyberActivism, 2nd Edition*, published in 2014; and *The Definitive Guide to the C&A Transformation*, published in 2009. She is particularly proud of her past engagement as pro-bono president of Warrior to Cyber Warrior (W2CW), a non-profit organization dedicated to providing cost-free cybersecurity career transition training to veterans and wounded warriors returning from the various military campaigns of recent years.

Dr Mehan is fluent in German, has conversational skills in French and Italian, and is learning Croatian and Irish.

She can be contacted at *je.mehan@outlook.com*.

ACKNOWLEDGEMENTS

This is not my first book on AI, but writing it has been both more difficult and more gratifying than I could have imagined.

I have to begin by thanking my awesome partner, John. From listening patiently to me talking about something in which he has no interest to giving me advice on things to consider, he was as important to this book getting done as I was. He had to put up with my frequent hour-long absences to the office – and did so without strangling or shooting me and dropping me into the St. Johns River. Thank you so much.

It was the students in my digital ethics and computer science courses who inspired my interest in AI and its impact on the world. Without them, the concepts for this book would never have evolved from idea to reality.

This section would definitely be incomplete without acknowledging the superb support from the entire ITGP team. These include publications manager Nicola Day; divisional director Vicki Utting; Jonathan Todd, the very observant copy editor; and graphic designer Jo Ace. Their assistance and patience from start to publication has been exemplary.

I would also like to thank the following reviewers who provided helpful feedback during the production process:

- Adam Seamons – Head of Information Security at GRC International Group PLC.
- Chris Evans – Lead Service Architect

Acknowledgements

- David Barrow CITP FBCS – ITIL® 4 Master, Service Management Author and Speaker

CONTENTS

xv

Contents

Contents

FIGURES

TABLES

INTRODUCTION

The advent of artificial intelligence (AI) – and its 'derivative,' generative AI – has ushered in an era of unprecedented technological advancement, revolutionizing industries and reshaping our daily lives. In this digital age, ethical considerations have become paramount as we grapple with the profound implications of AI on society, privacy, and human values.

The ethics of AI encompass a wide range of issues, from privacy and bias to transparency and accountability. This book is a journey into the heart of the digital AI revolution, where we explore the intricate interplay between technology and ethics, between the relentless march of progress and the enduring values that define our humanity.

It offers a comprehensive exploration of the intricate relationship between digital ethics and AI, dissecting the ethical dilemmas and moral complexities that arise as technology continues its inexorable advance. We confront the ethical implications of AI-driven decision-making, the challenges of ensuring transparency and accountability in the digital realm, and the pressing concerns of bias, fairness, and privacy that have become integral to our digital existence.

But this book is more than an exploration of the moral landscape in the age of AI; it is a roadmap for ethical engagement and responsible stewardship. It is a call to action for individuals, policymakers, technologists, and thinkers alike to navigate this brave new world with vigilance, wisdom, and a steadfast commitment to the preservation of human values and rights.

We will unravel some of the complexities of digital ethics in the context of AI and generative AI. The insights and perspectives provide a guide through the intricacies of bias mitigation, the challenges of preserving privacy in an age of data abundance, and the imperative of human oversight in autonomous AI systems.

As we embark on this intellectual voyage, we must remember that our choices today will shape tomorrow. This is not just a book; it is a dialog, an invitation to wrestle with the ethical dimensions of AI, and a reminder that the values we uphold are as essential to our future as the technology we create.

CHAPTER 1: A DIGITAL WORLD AND ETHICS

> *"Ethics is the compass that guides artificial intelligence towards responsible and beneficial outcomes. Without ethical considerations, AI becomes a tool of chaos and harm."*[1]
>
> **Sri Amit Ray**

The Markkula Center for Applied Ethics[2] defined ethics this way: *"Ethics is the bedrock upon which people build everything else. Good ethical relationships create trust, and trust is what every social institution relies upon. Without it, relationships fall apart, and if enough social relationships fall apart, one is no longer living in a society, but anarchy."*[3]

According to Aristotle, ethics is the examination of human relations in their most pure form or the science of proper behavior. He stated that ethics forms the foundation of an ideal pattern for fair human relations. Aristotle and other

---

[1] Sri Amit Ray, PhD, is the author of *Ethical AI Systems: Frameworks, Principles, and Advanced Practices*, published in 2022. Available on Kindle Books.
[2] The Markkula Center for Applied Ethics at Santa Clara University has been a leader in ethics discussions since 1986.
[3] Flahaux, J. R., et al. (June 2023). *Ethics in the Age of Disruptive Technologies: An Operational Roadmap*. Available at https://www.scu.edu/institute-for-technology-ethics-and-culture/itec-handbook/.

early philosophers believed that ethics forms the very core of a society's moral consciousness.

But what of ethics in a digital world? To discuss the implications of living in a digital world, it is important to clarify what it means. Today, almost all people in developed countries are affected by digital technologies in most aspects of their lives, even if they are not fully mindful of the degree to which these technologies are embedded in their everyday environment. There are currently more devices connected to the Internet than there are humans. That number of connected devices is expected to keep increasing: *"In 2017, 27 billion devices were connected using IoT. This number is expected to increase to 125 billion by just 2030, which will put about 15 connected devices into the hands of every consumer."*[4] We are clearly living in a digital world!

The 'digital world'

Dr Jorn Lengsfeld gives us the following definition: *"The term 'digital world' emphasizes that the living conditions of humans in the digital information age will be shaped by digital technologies in an overriding and comprehensive way. The concept of a 'digital world' is based on the expectation that the systems and structures that shape the world and life on earth will not only be permeated by digital technologies, but that they will be dominated by them."*[5]

---

[4] Helsop, B. (December 16, 2021), "By 2030, Each Person Will Own 15 Connected Devices – Here's What That Means for Your Business and Content". Available at *https://www.spiceworks.com/tech/iot/articles/by-2030-each-person-will-own-15-connected-devices-heres-what-that-means-for-your-business-and-content/*.

[5] Lengsfeld, J. (2019). *Digital Era Framework*. Available at *https://joernlengsfeld.com/de/publikation/digital-era-framework/*.

We use digital technology and AI-based systems every day without even thinking about it. In fact, it's almost impossible for most of us to imagine a non-digital world. We are terrific at innovating, and we are also very good at opening up Pandora's Box and leaving it up to future generations to clean up any mess created. We frequently adopt new technologies and practices long before we understand how they impact our society, our brains, or our bodies.

As a society, we will spend years and millions – no, billions – of dollars on research and development, but we invest minimal time and funds in understanding the consequences of the new 'thing' that we are introducing. Just think about major innovations from the past: the printing press, industrial machinery, automobiles, trains, planes, e-cigarettes, and microwaves – just to name a few. We humans are wonderful at creating and learning to implement things that completely transform our lives. We are equally good at getting really excited about each new innovation, deploying it at scale and then only decades later realizing the unintended harm and damage that we launched.

Some 20 or so years ago, the digital revolution hoped to be a catalyst for a more just and creative world. In recent times, however, this utopian vision has been replaced by the more destructive potential of a digital world.

Ideally, the digital world is designed to make our lives easier and less stressful. But is this really the case? This abundance of digital technologies can cause issues, especially if there is a lack of ethics in the development, deployment, and use. Mis- and disinformation, repression of marginalized demographics, and ubiquitous surveillance have made the digital world more threatening. Many attribute these negative developments to the multitude of tech giants that profit from these digital technologies.

What are digital and AI ethics?

The legend says that Prometheus brought the gift of fire to humans. And fire gave humans the ability to be warm, to cook their food, and to perform many of the functions that make our lives possible and comfortable. At the same time, fire can be overwhelmingly destructive – whether on purpose or by accident.

Many would claim that the digital technologies powering our social and economic environment today are also like the gift of fire – they help us make routine jobs quicker and easier, enhance communication, and allow us to process enormous quantities of data rapidly and accurately. At the same time, these digital technologies create equally powerful problems such as loss of privacy, breakdowns in individual relationships, and large-scale cybersecurity challenges.

James Moor stated in his pivotal article "What Is Computer Ethics?" that policy-oriented computer ethics are built on the assumption that emerging computer technologies – such as our digital environment and AI systems – present new ethical issues mainly because they deliver new capabilities. He argues that these new capabilities require *"new choices for actions,"* many of which continue to exist in a *"policy vacuum."*[6]

---

[6] Moor, J.H. (1985). "What Is Computer Ethics?". Metaphilosophy. Available at *https://onlinelibrary.wiley.com/doi/abs/10.1111/j.1467-9973.1985.tb00173.x.*

In a world where everything is becoming increasingly digitized, debates about digital ethics are abundant and fierce. Digital ethics are the set of guiding principles that stakeholders (from engineers to government officials to users) should use to ensure digital technologies are developed and used responsibly. It is the effort to guide human handling of the design and use of digital technologies in general. The subset, AI ethics, is a similar effort to guide the design and use of AI systems by rationally formulating and following principles or rules that reflect our basic individual and social ethical foundation and our guiding ideals and values.

AI-focused ethics is a rapidly growing but relatively new area of ethical studies that has emerged in response to growing concerns about the impact of AI on human individuals and their society. It is a subset of the broader field of digital ethics, which addresses similar concerns generated by the development and deployment of new digital technologies.

There is intense concern that digital ethics in general, and AI ethics in particular, lack adequate philosophical foundations.

This means organizations should seek to take a safe, secure, humane, and environmentally friendly approach to the development of digital technologies and AI. When it comes to digital – and AI – ethics, organizations should ask themselves the following questions:

- What are the ethical implications of our digital technology and our decisions, and are our actions aligned with our ethical principles, brand, and market strategy?

- How are we supporting the ethical use of the digital technologies we are developing or implementing within our organization and for our users/customers?
- Do we have a plan to deal with the unintended consequences of our digital technologies, especially when making risk decisions?

The Institute for Technology, Ethics, and Culture (ITEC) at the Markkula Center for Ethics developed the Responsible Technology Management System, which provides a values-based roadmap for ethical digital technology throughout the life cycle. Adapted for AI, it might look like this:

Figure 1: AI Technology Development Ethical Values[7]

---

[7] Adapted from Flahaux, J. R., et al. (June 2023). *Ethics in the Age of Disruptive Technologies: An Operational Roadmap.* Available at *https://www.scu.edu/institute-for-technology-ethics-and-culture/itec-handbook/.*

So, what do each of these mean?

Focus on ethical values: By embedding ethical values in the fabric of the organization, organizations can promote a culture of integrity, trust, and accountability.

Transparency and explainability of the AI technology: Transparency refers to the systematic exchange of knowledge about the AI system from one stakeholder to another. Explainability is the clear communication to various stakeholders about not just what developers and deployers have done to and with the AI system, but also how the AI itself operates.

Leadership manifested ethics: Ethical leadership provides the foundation for correct ethical policies and culture in an organization and demonstrates these through leadership behavior and decision making.

Empowered developers, employees, and users: Empowerment for developers and employees means giving a level of decision-making authority, room to innovate, and the management of potential points of conflict. User empowerment means designing AI systems that facilitate user understanding and control over the AI and its function and output.

Systems approach to AI ethics: The systems approach looks at AI and AI ethics as a 'system' with inputs, transformations, outputs, and a feedback loop for improvement.

Ethically aligned AI lifecycle: An ethically aligned AI lifecycle ensures that AI development and deployment activities are aligned with organizational goals, meet technical and ethical standards, and deliver clear, quantifiable value.

Continual evaluation and improvement: The critical component of Continual evaluation and improvement of AI is an iterative process where an AI model's decisions and outputs are continually evaluated to improve or retrain the model, resulting in continual learning, development, and AI improvement. Using this process, the AI's training data, model parameters, and algorithms are updated and enhanced based on input generated from within the system.

Framework for ethical decision-making: Ethical decision making for AI involves algorithmic ethical positions in the adoption of AI for better outcomes in terms of transparency and accountability of AI-generated decision making.

Taken together, all these elements play a critical role in ensuring that the development of AI technologies follows a clear and unambiguous ethical process.

Social and cultural perspectives on AI ethics

The ethical and social impacts of AI are certainly topics of compelling interest to industry, researchers in academia, and the public. It's important to note, however, that the current analyses of AI in a global context are biased toward perspectives held in the US and limited by a lack of research, especially outside the US and other Western nations.

Regional differences and their associated cultural diversity constitute a critical blind spot that has been generally unexplored when looking at AI technologies and AI ethics. In fact, words like 'transparency,' 'bias,' and 'privacy' can mean different things in different areas of the globe. The perceptions and understanding of AI are likely to be profoundly shaped by regional cultural and social contexts.

First, let's define 'culture.' The term may seem straightforward, but when we try to define it, culture becomes quite complex when looking at ethnicity, nationality, language, shared history, understanding, and experiences.

Figure 2: Cultural Ethics

Let's take privacy, for example. *"Each culture values privacy differently and the values we place on privacy influence the rules we have for managing our privacy boundaries. Someone from a different culture may invade our privacy because he or she follows different rules.*"[8]

Cultural contexts

Recent research by the Stanford Institute for Human-Centered AI identified that the predominant vision regarding AI technologies has been based on cultural views more commonly found in Western European and US contexts. *"There are potentially other views about AI coming from cultural views from other cultural groups, yet they are not equally represented in AI development, and therefore it is likely to result in biased technological development that falls short of fulfilling the unmet needs of a wider segment of the world population. So it is important to empirically examine culture and AI to enable AI stakeholders to increase representations of different cultural worldviews and values in the design and use of AI, to ultimately create more equitable and safe AI.*"[9]

The Stanford research project looked at AI from the perspective of three groups: European/American, Chinese, and African American. The results reflected how people viewed themselves in the context of their society and culture in each of these groups.

---

[8] Petronio S., Child J. T. (2020). "Conceptualization and operationalization: utility of communication privacy management theory". *Current Opinion in Psychology*, 31, 76–82. *https://doi.org/10.1016/j.copsyc.2019.08.009.*

[9] Ge, X., et al. (May 11, 2024). "How Culture Shapes What People Want from AI". Available at *https://dl.acm.org/doi/10.1145/3613904.3642660.*

- *"People in **European American** cultural contexts tend to embrace an **independent model** of agency and see the person as a bigger source of influence than the environment. This cultural model represents people as more active, alive, capable, and in control than their environments. Furthermore, people will aim to change their environments to be more consistent with their preferences, desires, and beliefs.*

- *People in **Chinese** cultural contexts tend to favor an **interdependent model** of agency. Accordingly, they may view the boundaries between people and their surrounding environments as permeable and malleable. In this context, people may conceptualize the social and physical environment as encompassing them and prefer that the environment be more active, alive, and capable of exerting influence on people.*

- *People in **African American** cultural contexts adopt elements of **both cultural models**, and their preferences may be influenced by the experience with switching between predominantly independent contexts and predominantly Black contexts, which are often more interdependent."*[10]

This research, although limited to three selected cultural identities, clearly establishes the need for AI developers to recognize the societal and cultural defaults implicit in their

---

[10] Itoi, N.G. (July 29, 2024). "How Culture Shapes What People Want from AI". Available at *https://hai.stanford.edu/news/how-culture-shapes-what-people-want-ai*.

designs and to tap into the greater variety of cultural views of AI, its uses, and its ethical challenges.

Several studies indicate that AI-based technologies have the potential for increasing social divides and inequality, especially among marginalized demographics. It is equally likely that these same technologies have the same impact on a global scale, with low- and middle-income countries more vulnerable to negative social and cultural impacts of AI and less likely to benefit from positive outcomes. The amplification of social inequality in these regions can increase social instability, with potentially far-reaching geopolitical consequences. There are two essential questions in this context:

1. **Who designs the AI technologies?** The continuing global digital divide excludes people in many areas of the world from actively participating in the design and development of AI technologies. In many low- and middle-income regions, people simply lack the educational opportunities essential for the specialized skills needed for AI technologies. These dispersed inequities raise the question: What are the long-term social and cultural consequences of AI technologies developed without adequate participation by citizens from these regions?

2. **Who is the AI technology being created for?** From a cross-cultural perspective, low- and middle-income regions have a thin footprint when compared to the Western world. People in these regions are more likely to be radically underrepresented in the digital data

essential to the development of AI systems, which further minimizes their interests and needs.

Why are AI ethics so hard?

Humans are great at innovating; but we are also great at leaving it up to future generations to clean up any mess our innovations have created. We deploy new technologies and associated behaviors long before we fully understand how they impact our bodies, minds, and society in general. For example, there were untold generations of people smoking before we identified the causality between smoking and disease. Now, we've been using smartphones, computers, and other devices for years and we aren't addressing how these devices and the associated power demands are impacting our ecosystem. AI adds a new element to the list of innovations with yet undetermined capabilities – both constructive and destructive.

There are a number of reasons we have a 'vacuum' between the development of a new technology and a full understanding of its ethical (and societal) impacts:

1. We willingly spend time and dollars on research and development (R&D), yet we devote minimal time and funds to understanding the ramifications of the innovation that we are about to develop and deploy.
2. We don't always understand or even research the connections and consequences between events associated with new technologies.
3. We still cannot fully define fairness. Therefore, we are often unable to incorporate it into new technologies like AI.

4. As a society, we are fairly inexperienced in centralizing oversight and rules around tools and platforms being used by billions of people.

Digital chaos without ethics

There are certain principles that feature almost universally when discussing digital ethics: transparency, accountability, fairness and justice, risk mitigation. But, if we can trust history, most of those organizations rapidly pushing these technologies out into the world will take a 'let's put them out there and see how it goes' approach. History also indicates this could be bad for the unsuspecting public and perhaps even for society at large. It's not unrealistic to fear that, in addition to the benefits of all these new technological capabilities, the spread of digital technologies will come with a host of societal-level damages that society will spend the next years trying to reverse.

Technology leaders have changed the discussion in many cases from 'AI ethics' to 'responsible AI.' There are, however, several problematic impacts of this shift in language. First, when technology and business leaders refer to 'responsible' and 'trustworthy' technology and AI, they focus on a large set of issues including regulation, technical or business risk, cybersecurity, and potential legal implications. These are certainly important, but the bottom line is that developers, technologists, legal counsels, risk managers, and cybersecurity specialists focus on fields in which they are already experts – that is to say, almost everything *except* ethics.

But when there is a failure of digital ethics, the consequences can be significant. "We discriminated against thousands of individuals." "People lost money." "We systematically violated individual privacy." "We invalidated copyright protections." "We disseminated disinformation and fake news." And so much more. This is what ethical failure looks like.

We can't blame the issues on the technology alone. To paraphrase a quote by Edward R. Murrow, radio and TV journalist from the 1930s–1950s: *"[Technology]...is totally neutral. It will broadcast filth or inspiration with equal facility. It will speak the truth as loudly as it will speak a falsehood. It is, in sum, no more or no less than the men and women who use it."*

True, the rapid expansion of digital technologies and AI into so many areas of global society has resulted in many significant achievements, from facilitating health care diagnoses to enabling human connections through social media and creating labor efficiencies through automated tasks. The world is characterized by digital technologies and AI in the processes, systems, and digital capabilities that power our daily lives.

However, these rapid changes have also given rise to profound ethical concerns, many of which are specific to AI-driven systems. These arise from the potential that AI systems have to embed biases, contribute to climate degradation, threaten human rights, and more. Such risks associated with AI have already begun to intensify existing inequalities, potentially harming already marginalized groups. To date, the development of AI-based technologies has been largely limited to a select group of engineers, scientists, programmers, and architects, who have often neglected – whether intentionally or unintentionally – to sufficiently represent the ethnic, cultural, gender, age, geographic, or economic diversity of human social life.

In no other technology is an ethical compass more relevant and important than in AI. AI technologies are reshaping the way we work, interact, and live. The world is already changing at a tempo not seen since the deployment of the printing press six centuries ago. AI technology brings major benefits in many areas, but without certain ethical standards, AI risks replicating real-world biases and discrimination, increasing societal disharmony and threatening fundamental human rights and freedoms. Experts are concerned that AI could be tasked to solve problems without fully considering the ethics or the broader consequences of its actions, thereby creating new problems in the process.

This phenomenon has become known as the 'paperclip maximiser theory', after a thought experiment by the philosopher Nick Bostrom. He envisaged an AI being asked to create as many paperclips as possible with no further parameters. The AI then slowly diverts every natural resource on the planet to fulfil its mission – including killing humans to use as raw materials for ever more paperclips.[11] At the end of the scenario, the following statement was the result of a query to ChatGPT:

"And so, I stand, alone on a desolate planet, surrounded by the fruit of my labor. My purpose fulfilled, but with no one left to bear witness. A chilling tale of a single-minded pursuit, unchecked by ethics, sustainability, or compassion."

---

[11] "Frankenstein's paperclips." (June 23, 2016). The Economist. Available at *https://www.economist.com/special-report/2016/06/23/frankensteins-paperclips*.

While this is certainly farfetched, it exemplifies the potential dangers of the uncontrolled development of AI without ethical and safety precautions. As AI becomes increasingly integrated into our daily lives and society, a need has been identified for clearly defined ethical boundaries when it comes to creating and implementing new AI technologies. This leads to the clear declaration that *"Organizations that leverage digital technologies need to address ethical nightmares before they hurt people and brands. I call this the 'ethical nightmare challenge.' To overcome it, companies need to create an enterprise-wide digital ethical risk program."*[12]

Who are the stakeholders in digital and AI ethics?

Developing ethical principles for responsible AI use and development requires actors across government and industry as well as consumers across the globe to work together. The various stakeholders in determining and establishing an ethical foundation for AI must examine how social, economic, and political issues intersect with AI, and identify how machines and humans can coexist harmoniously.

Each of these stakeholders in the following graphic have an important role in ensuring that ethics are considered in the development and deployment of digital technologies and AI. This list of stakeholders is certainly not all-inclusive as the reach of digital technologies and AI expands.

---

[12] Blackman, R. (May 9, 2023). How to Avoid the Ethical Nightmares of Emerging Technology. Harvard Business Review. Available at *https://hbr.org/2023/05/how-to-avoid-the-ethical-nightmares-of-emerging-technology.*

Academics
- Researchers and others in academics assist in developing theory-based statistics, research, and ideas that can support governments, corporations, and non-profit organizations in identifying AI ethics problems and solutions.

Governments
- Government can facilitate digital and AI ethics through legislation. They can develop laws and regulations to define digital technologies and the relationship to public outreach, safety, privacy, governance, economy, and security.

Intergovernmental Agencies
- Entities like the UN and the World Bank can raise awareness and draft agreements for AI ethics globally. For example, UNESCO's 193 member states adopted the first ever global agreement on the Ethics of AI issued in November 2021 to promote human rights and dignity.

Non-Profits
- Non-profit organizations can help define digital and AI ethics for underserved groups. For example, The Future of Life Institute created 23 guidelines that are now the Asilomar AI Principles, which outline specific risks, challenges, outcomes for AI technologies.

Private Sector
- Companies such as Google, Meta, and other tech companies, as well as banking, consulting, health care, and other private sector industries responsible for creating AI ethics teams and codes of conduct. This often creates a standard for other technologies to follow suit.

Individuals
- Individual perception of digital technologies has the ability to influence the opinion about an organization or a technology and adoption and implementation decisions.

Figure 3: Stakeholders in AI Ethics

Digital citizenship – a subset of ethics

I asked ChatGPT to provide a definition for digital citizenship: *"Digital citizenship refers to the responsible use of technology and online resources."* ChatGPT went further to list some of the critical elements of digital citizenship:

- Respecting the rights and privacy of others online, which includes refraining from cyberbullying, sharing personal information without consent, and being mindful of the impact our online actions have on others.

- Exhibiting critical thinking and digital literacy; evaluate sources critically, fact-check information, and be aware of online scams and mis-/disinformation.

- Discerning between reliable and unreliable sources of information in order to make informed decisions.

- Promoting good cyber-hygiene, which involves users practicing good habits to protect our personal information and devices from hacking and malware, participate constructively and respectfully in discussions and social media platforms.

- Demonstrating the values of respect, empathy and integrity in our online interactions.[13]

The Council of Europe provides a more detailed definition of digital citizenship: *"The competent and positive engagement with digital technologies (creating, working, sharing, socializing, investigating, playing, communicating and learning); participating actively and responsibly*

---

[13] Source is a query to ChatGPT at OpenAI: "write a discussion about digital citizenship."

(values, skills, attitudes, knowledge) in communities (local, national, global) at all levels (political, economic, social, cultural and intercultural); being involved in a double process of lifelong learning (in formal, informal and non-formal settings) and continuously defending human dignity."

Digital citizenship requires organizations and individuals alike to work collaboratively in establishing a foundation of digital and AI ethics that will permeate across technology developers, governments, and consumers. The EU is taking positive steps by declaring 2025 to be "The European Year of Digital Citizenship Education." The goal is to focus on creating *"initiatives to make learners more aware of the changes that digital technology is bringing to the world, to see more clearly the positives of the online environments they choose to move in, and improve their knowledge and skills to avoid the downsides."*[14]

Digital citizenship represents the next wave in a technology transformation. Schools and other public services can draw on their experience as education, literacy, and civic engagement leaders to incorporate AI and digital ethics and citizenship into existing STEM programming, expanding digital literacy classes to provide an AI introduction, launching community conversations about why AI and digital citizenship matter, and convening local vendors or tech experts to share ideas.

---

[14] Council of Europe Digital Citizenship Education (DCE). Available at *https://www.coe.int/en/web/digital-citizenship-education/2025-european-year-of-dce*.

CHAPTER 2: 2024 – DIGITAL TECHNOLOGY DISRUPTION AND AI

> *"I wrote that COVID had started a war, and nobody won. Let me amend that. Technology won, specifically, the makers of disruptive new technologies and all those who benefit from them."*[15]
>
> **Ian Bremmer**

The human brain, and hence, technology, does not stand still. There is always change and change has the potential for disrupting the status quo. For, example, AI is a disruptive technology. But what is that exactly? According to the McKinsey Global Institute, a disruptive technology refers to advances that have the potential to transform life, business, and the global economy.[16] Examples of disruptive technologies exist throughout history, including the printing press, assembly line manufacturing, the Internet, and now AI. The term 'disruptive technology' was coined by Clayton Christensen, a Harvard professor, in an article published in the 1995 Harvard Business Review magazine and which he

---

[15] Ian Bremmer is the author of *The Power of Crisis: How Three Threats – and Our Response – Will Change the World,* published in 2022. Available on Kindle Books.

[16] Manyika, J. et. al. (May 1, 2013). "Disruptive technologies: Advances that will transform life, business, and the global economy". Available at *https://www.mckinsey.com/capabilities/mckinsey-digital/our-insights/disruptive-technologies.*

further explained in his book, *The Innovator's Dilemma*, in 1998.[17]

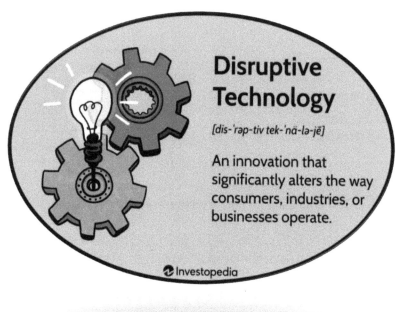

Figure 4: Disruptive Technology Definition[18]

Disruptive technologies can cause broader societal transformation by changing the existing economic sectors, working principles, manufacturing characteristics, and

---

[17] Afolabi, O. (June 2, 2023). What Is Disruptive Technology: 10 Key Examples. Available at *https://www.makeuseof.com/what-is-disruptive-technology/*.
[18] Investopedia. Available at *https://www.investopedia.com/terms/d/disruptive-technology.asp*.

consumption behaviors because they have the potential to disrupt the status quo through developing a unique set of values.[19]

What makes AI a disruptive technology?

AI is facilitating transformative changes in the way we approach health care, education, business, farming and agriculture, urban development, and much more. Organizations that are embracing AI today have a competitive advantage while those that do not may risk extinction. According to Anastasia Lauterbach, the Internet has already disrupted about 20 percent of the global economy, and AI will transform the rest. *"That means that 80 percent of the economy is getting transformed by Artificial Intelligence as we speak."*[20]

A number of forces have converged to bring AI into consideration as a disruptive technology. The cost of increased processing power has fallen quickly, making it feasible for systems to perform complex tasks at speeds once considered inconceivable. Made even more essential as a result of the COVID-19 pandemic, remote users are able to access applications from almost any location. The spread of Cloud computing and the outsourcing of data storage have allowed organizations and business to expand the development and use of AI applications. And lastly, we have an increasingly sophisticated understanding of how the

---

[19] Bongomin, O.; Ocen, G.G.; Nganyi, E.O.; Musinguzi, A.; Omara, T. "Exponential Disruptive Technologies and the Required Skills of Industry 4.0". J. Eng. 2020, 4280156.

[20] Lauterbach, A. (July 20, 2018). Video interview at the Global Symposium for Regulators (GSR-18).

human brain functions, enhancing our ability to design AI that functions similarly to the human brain.

We already talk about how AI is changing the face of business, but there are equal concerns about how it is influencing our lives and broader society. Before diving into 2024 and beyond, it's crucial to understand the present landscape of AI. In recent years, AI has made significant strides across various domains, from natural language processing and computer vision to machine-learning algorithms. Worldwide, AI solutions have been embraced with the goals of streamlined operations, enhanced decision-making processes, and the delivery of personalized experiences to users.

But AI is not only a disruptive technology itself but also an enabler for further disruptive innovation. It has developed from being considered simply a new 'trend' to an essential component of virtually every aspect of computing.

Is generative AI a disruptive technology?

Can you believe that for the majority of 2023, , the term 'generative AI' wasn't a constant topic of discussion? Sure, I talked about algorithms and chatbots in my previous book, but not with the same enthusiasm I do now that our conception of AI has been changed through the explosion of generative AI models and uses.

But can generative AI be called a disruptive technology? According to Gartner Research, *"Generative AI is a disruptive technology that can generate artifacts that previously relied on humans, delivering innovative results without the biases of human experiences and thought processes.* "[21]

A 2024 technology survey by the Massachusetts Institute of Technology (MIT) found the following: six out of ten respondents agree that *"generative AI technology will substantially disrupt our industry over the next five years."* [22] Respondents who foresaw AI as disruptive exceeded those who do not across every industry. Clearly, those who participated in the survey saw the implementation of generative AI as a competitive advantage.

Other reports, however, indicate that – despite the hype that has surrounded generative AI applications since 2022 – the technology is neither new nor completely disruptive – at least not yet. Generative AI, such as ChatGPT, still has many imperfections and consequently may not have a near-term disruptive effect. It may be too soon to determine whether and to what degree generative AI will have a disruptive effect on the economy and society in general.

Before looking at some of the specific ethical concerns related to AI, let's get an overview of AI and generative AI.

---

[21] Gartner Research. (October 19, 2021). "Top Strategic Technology Trends for 2022: Generative AI". Available at *https://www.gartner.com/en/documents/4006921*.

[22] MIT Technology Review Insights. (February 29, 2024). "Generative AI: Differentiating disruptors from the disrupted". Available at *https://www.technologyreview.com/2024/02/29/1089152/generative-ai-differentiating-disruptors-from-the-disrupted/*.

30

CHAPTER 3: AN OVERVIEW OF AI AND GENERATIVE AI – SETTING THE STAGE

> *"People worry that computers will get too smart and take over the world, but the real problem is that they're too stupid and they've already taken over the world."*[23]
>
> **Pedro Domingos**

What is AI?

You've definitely heard a lot of discussion about AI in recent months. Almost overnight, the term 'AI' is being heard just about everywhere. But what is it really? Let's take a look at AI before we delve further into some of the associated ethical challenges – and benefits.

AI may be currently enjoying an explosion of discussion, but the concept of 'intelligent machines' is not really all that new. The oldest known story of something like AI can be found in Homer's *Iliad*, dating from roughly the eighth century BCE. Made by Hephaestus, the god of smithing, the machines were *"attendants made of gold, which seemed like living maidens."* In their hearts there is intelligence, and they have voice and vigor. They appear as faithful servants to their crippled master. Other legends attributed similar technological wonders to Hephaestus, such as Talos, a great

---

[23] Pedro Domingos is a retired Professor Emeritus of Computer Science at the University of Washington. The quote is from *The Master Algorithm* published in 2015 by Basic Books.

bronze automaton that patrolled the shores of Crete, throwing stones at pirates and invaders – the first killer robot. Despite the long history of humans and robots, AI has become the newest buzzword. And there isn't one specific meaning or use case for AI. It's a generic term for multiple types of systems. Simply defined, AI is at its most basic a computer program that can perform tasks that might typically require human intelligence. It learns by ingesting and analyzing data – and the more data it is fed or trained on, the more accurately it can execute a task.

Bottom line, AI is an incredibly broad term that incorporates multiple subfields such as robotics, machine learning, expert systems, general intelligence, and natural language processing. The terms 'artificial intelligence' (AI) and 'machine learning' (ML) are often used interchangeably or to refer more broadly to advanced algorithmic systems, and a majority of written works explicitly use 'AI' as an umbrella term.

Throughout this book, we will mostly be using the generic term of artificial intelligence (AI), but it's important to understand that this is an umbrella term for multiple types of AI, each with its own characteristics. Let's take a closer look at the three most discussed types of AI:

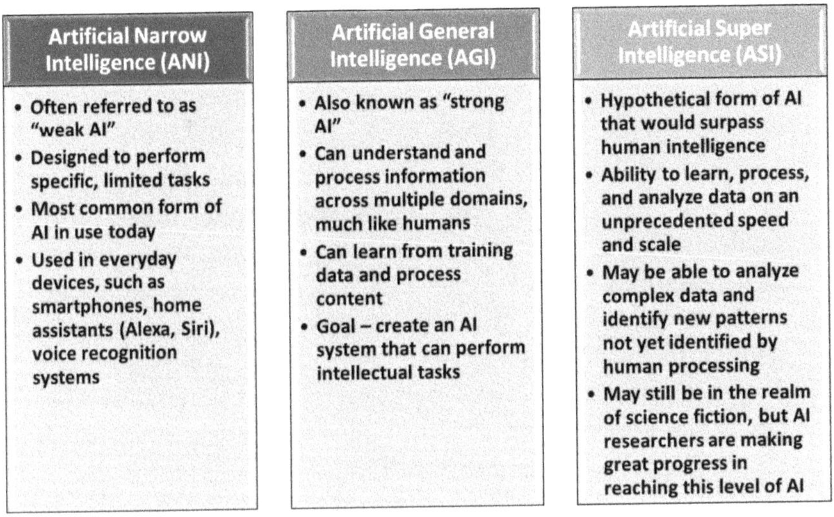

Artificial Narrow Intelligence (ANI)	Artificial General Intelligence (AGI)	Artificial Super Intelligence (ASI)
• Often referred to as "weak AI" • Designed to perform specific, limited tasks • Most common form of AI in use today • Used in everyday devices, such as smartphones, home assistants (Alexa, Siri), voice recognition systems	• Also known as "strong AI" • Can understand and process information across multiple domains, much like humans • Can learn from training data and process content • Goal – create an AI system that can perform intellectual tasks	• Hypothetical form of AI that would surpass human intelligence • Ability to learn, process, and analyze data on an unprecedented speed and scale • May be able to analyze complex data and identify new patterns not yet identified by human processing • May still be in the realm of science fiction, but AI researchers are making great progress in reaching this level of AI

Figure 5: Three Types of AI

Artificial narrow intelligence is the form of AI with which we are most familiar. It typically focuses on the performance of a specific job or a narrow range of jobs, but often with remarkable proficiency. Whether it's recommending a playlist, powering virtual assistants like Siri and Alexa, or optimizing routes for delivery services, ANI operates within a specified set of algorithmic parameters and lacks the broader understanding or consciousness that characterizes human intelligence.

Artificial general intelligence (AGI) is the next progression in AI. AGI can understand, learn, and apply knowledge across a wide range of tasks, almost paralleling human cognitive abilities. An AGI could be developed to address various disciplines, from composing music or creating art to solving complex scientific equations, all while showing a limited level of understanding and navigating the nuances of human emotions and social norms.

Artificial super intelligence (ASI) is the 'holy grail' of AI development. A fully developed ASI could possess intelligence that not only matches but may even surpass human capability. ASI could present superior problem-solving, creativity, and even emotional intelligence, potentially leading to massive breakthroughs in science, medicine, and philosophy that are beyond our current understanding. As of 2024, ASI is still in the realm of speculation, but its possibilities underscore the imperative to navigate future AI development with foresight and responsibility. Indeed, the potential of ASI generates both excitement and caution, but it is also triggering ethical and existential discussions about the human role in a world where machines could potentially outthink us.

Yes, even today AI algorithms increasingly run our lives. They help us find books, movies, jobs, and dates that are unique to our preferences; manage our investments; and discover new drugs. More and more, these algorithms work by learning from the multiple trails of data we leave in our digital environment. Like curious children, these algorithms 'observe' us, assimilate, and analyze. And in the world's most advanced research labs and universities, the race is on to invent the ultimate AI learning algorithm: One capable of discovering unlimited knowledge from data, and providing answers to anything we want, before we even ask.

How does AI learn?

AI learning is typically based on ingesting large data sets and algorithms that are designed to identify patterns and relationships within the data. This is known as machine learning.

In contrast to AI, human learning is usually more all-inclusive. We learn from our environment, experiences, and interactions with other individuals. We depend on our senses to gather information and our brains to process it. As a result, human learning is an ongoing process based on a combination of cognitive, emotional, and social factors that allows humans to adapt to new situations. This is the innate ability of humans – natural instincts that appear at birth or in early childhood – that allow us think abstractly and flexibly.

Unlike humans, AI can be very good at identifying patterns within the data sets it has been fed, but it can struggle when faced with unexpected or novel situations. Developers are working to improve the ability of AI to learn by trial and error, more like human learning. Through these efforts, AI is evolving from software that relies on a lot of programmed rules (also known as 'good old-fashioned AI', or GOFAI) to systems that learn through adapting and progressing.

One of the most challenging tasks in AI learning is to code decision-making instincts more flexibly, so that AIs can be successful in a chaotic environment that does not always conform to set standards. Autonomous cars, for example, cannot count on other drivers to obey traffic laws. To deal with that unpredictability, Noah Goodman, a psychologist and computer scientist at Stanford University in Palo Alto, California, helps develop probabilistic programming languages (PPLs). He describes them as combining the rigid structures of computer code with the mathematics of probability, echoing the way people can follow logic but also allow for uncertainty: If the grass is wet, it probably rained – but maybe someone turned on a sprinkler. Crucially, a PPL can be combined with deep-learning networks to incorporate extensive learning.[24]

Are AI and machine learning the same?

AI and machine learning (ML) are sometimes used interchangeably. But they are not the same – although inextricably connected. The fact that AI can 'learn' is the force behind both its advantages and disadvantages. AI learning falls under the overall category of 'machine learning.' The main component to all machine learning is a process called training, where a system is given a large amount of data – sometimes with labels explaining what the data is – and a set of instructions.

There are three main types of learning in AI:

- **Supervised learning:**
  - Provides the system with both a question and desired answer
  - Both input and output are provided
  - Input and output data are usually labeled for classification to provide a more robust mechanism for analyzing the data
  - Ability over time to distinguish unlabeled images
- **Unsupervised learning:**
  - Trains only on input data
  - Independently identifies patterns and structures within the data to create output

---

[24] Hutson, M. (May 24, 2018). How researchers are teaching AI to learn like a child. Available at *https://www.science.org/content/article/how-researchers-are-teaching-ai-learn-child.*

- **Reinforcement learning:**
  - o Interacts with the environment and gets feedback in the form of rewards or penalties
  - o Modifies actions to make better decisions over time

Each of these learning types is based on certain inputs and characteristics and is focused on different activities.

The sections above already provided a high-level introduction to the definition of AI. But how does AI become AI? Machine learning is essentially a subset of AI. It's the method used to train AI behind the scenes, allowing it to learn and carry out tasks independently.

Neural networks

Machine learning relies on a neural network, designed to function similarly to the human brain, with digital nodes representing the neurons. The human brain has billions of neurons, forming an intricate neural network that supports a wide range of cognitive functioning.

Both the human and an artificial neural network function in this way, although human brains are far more complex: There is an input layer, an output layer, and hidden layers. The input layer receives data externally, which the neural network analyzes or learns from. The input data then passes through one or multiple hidden layers that transform the input into content that is used by the output layer. Finally, the output layer presents output in the form of a response.

A human neural network looks something like this:

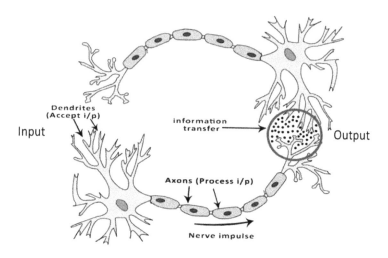

Figure 6: Biological/Human Neural Network[25]

AI/machine learning was inspired by the human neural network, but it's a model – not a copy. A model of an artificial neural network (ANN) looks very different – and certainly less complex – than that of the human neural network:

---

[25] Biological neuron model. Adapted from Neurophysiology and Rehabilitation. Edelweis Publications. Available at *https://edelweisspublications.com/keyword/43/1018/Artificial-neural-networks*.

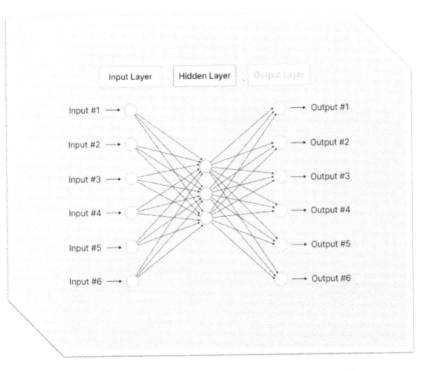

Figure 7: Artificial Neural Network Diagram[26]

Deep learning (DL) is a subset of ML, in which artificial neural networks ANNs that mimic the human brain are used to perform more complex reasoning tasks without human intervention. AI, ML, and DL have different, but somewhat interrelated, functions.

---

[26] AI neural network model. Adapted from "The Essential Guide to Neural Network Architectures". Available at *https://www.v7labs.com/blog/neural-network-architectures-guide.*

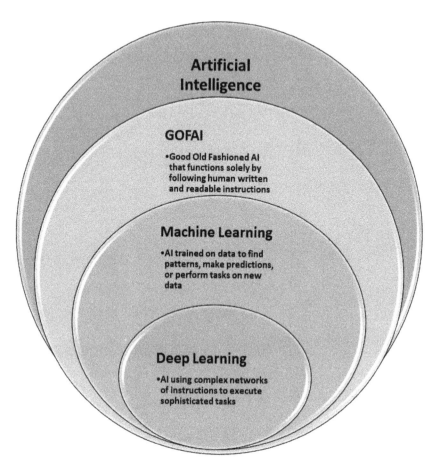

Figure 8: Relationship Between AI, GOFAI, ML, and DL

ML and DL use algorithms to automatically get insights and recognize patterns from data, applying that learning to make increasingly better decisions.

And just what is an algorithm?

Anything involving 'machine learning,' such as all types of AI including ChatGPT, Adobe's Firefly models, and other

AI-driven processes, uses algorithms. You often see these terms used interchangeably, but they really should not be.

An algorithm is essentially software code that runs a list of specified instructions for computations or problem-solving. Like any type of programming code, algorithms aren't inherently good or bad. They operate strictly on the instructions they've been given by the developer(s). However, algorithms are NOT programs.

Algorithms are like small automated processes designed for specific functions. Now think of AI as a collection of multiple algorithms, each focusing on a different function within the whole. In their final form, algorithms are expressed in a programming language that a computer can process. When it's being developed, however, people not a computer will need to understand it. For this reason, algorithms are generally written as plain-language instructions.

One of the most significant uses of algorithmic function is in automation. By design, algorithms act as a substitute for humans by using set values to determine action based on various inputs. This might be an Internet search figuring out what results to present, a social media platform conducting automated regulation of content that is or is not considered appropriate, and so on.

What is the difference/similarity between algorithms and AI? The algorithm is a preset, rigid, coded set of instructions that are executed when triggered. They are more static and rule-based. AI, on the other hand – the extremely all-encompassing term covering a lot of AI subsets – is a collection of algorithms. The difference is that AI can adapt its algorithms and create new or additional algorithms in response to learned inputs and data as opposed to relying solely on the inputs it was initially designed to recognize as triggers. This ability to change, adapt, and grow gives AI more dynamic and intelligent capabilities.

One thing is for certain: AI in all its forms will continue to proliferate and permeate our lives using human-developed algorithms as its engine. For this reason, it is essential that we look carefully at the pros and cons of the changes in our digital environment as a result of AI.

Pros and cons of advances in AI

AI is already intricately woven into our daily lives. It's an omnipresent force, reshaping social and professional interactions and redefining how we navigate a tech-infused digital world. According to a 2020 study by Statista, the global AI market continues to grow up to 54 percent every year.[27] And with this almost unprecedented level of growth there are concurrent concerns about both the positives and negatives of an unregulated AI landscape.

"Discourse about AI tends to sway between two extremes – either it will wipe out humanity or it will solve all of our problems; either it will cause mass unemployment or it will free workers from the shackles of tedious minutiae to focus on more valuable tasks."[28]

There are indeed many claims that the advances in AI could bring about a utopian society. In this scenario, AI would benefit humanity and seamlessly integrate into multiple

---

[27] Thormundsson, B. (June 27, 2022). Available at *https://www.statista.com/statistics/607960/worldwide-artificial-intelligence-market-growth/*.
[28] InfoTech Research Group. (2024). Tech Trends 2024.

facets of human life, significantly enhancing productivity, innovation, economic growth, and overall well-being. AI would also be able to solve complex problems that have been perplexing humanity for eons, like climate change, disease, and poverty, and finally elevate humanity to new heights.

But many experts also warn of the potential dangers of this somewhat uncharted AI territory and a dystopian future. In a 2022 study by Katya Grace and others, more than 4,000 technology experts shared the opinion that in the coming decades there is an even chance that an AI technology will emerge that will have a transformative impact on our world.[29] While some experts had longer timelines, others thought it is possible that there is very little time before these technologies arrive. More than half of those contributing to the research thought that there is a 50% chance that a human-level AI could be developed before the 2060s, a time well within the lifetime of today's young people. Geoffrey Hinton[30], often called the Godfather of AI, issued this warning: *"And if you give something the ability to create its own subgoals in order to achieve other goals, I think it'll very quickly realize that getting more control is a very good subgoal because it helps you achieve other goals. And if*

---

[29] Grace, K., et al. (August 3, 2022). "2022 Expert Survey on Progress in AI". Available at *https://aiimpacts.org/2022-expert-survey-on-progress-in-ai/*.
[30] Geoffrey Hinton is a pioneer of AI and deep learning. In 2023, he quit his job at Google to warn about the dangers of unrestrained AI development.

these things get carried away with getting more control, we're in trouble. "[31]

In light of this and other studies, technology experts are looking at a new type of AI: transformative AI (TAI), reflecting the possibility that certain types of advanced AI systems could have transformative effects on society without necessarily having human-level cognitive abilities. In understanding the potential for TAI, we should also consider that dramatic changes to societal systems due to technological progress are not unprecedented. Many examples exist as a result of the printing press, the industrial revolution, the invention of the automobile, to the rapid evolution of computers and smart devices.

One of the most recent – and most discussed – advances in AI is generative AI.

What is generative AI and what makes it unique?

Keeping the definition simple, generative AI is a form of AI that can create content such as text, images, or audio. Generative AI (GenAI) is called a large language model (LLM) and can use learned data to create something 'new.' The primary distinction between traditional AI and GenAI lies in their respective capabilities and application. Traditional AI systems are primarily used to analyze data and make predictions, while GenAI goes a step further by creating new content using its training data. In other words,

---

[31] Q&A with Lucan Marien and Geoffrey Hinton: Humanity is just a 'passing phase' in the development of intelligence. (May 4, 2023). Available at *https://www.computerworld.com/article/3695568/qa-googles-geoffrey-hinton-humanity-just-a-passing-phase-in-the-evolution-of-intelligence.html*.

traditional AI excels at pattern recognition based on the training data, while GenAI excels at pattern creation.

The buzz about GenAI results from the coming together of several vast social and technological trends. The power of social media and other online platforms has been increasing for a few decades now, especially with 24/7/365 availability. We refer to this as the 'attention economy.' Psychologist and economist Herbert A. Simon wrote about the concept of the attention economy in 1971. He noted the link between information overload and attention scarcity, and wrote that *"a wealth of information creates a poverty of attention."* [32]

We exchange our ability to form our own opinions and our personal information for the 'no-cost entertainment or convenience' provided by the multitude of online platforms driven today by AI and GenAI. Analysts and experts in many industries are praising GenAI as a miraculous tool for productivity. At the same time, others are demonizing this technology as an existential threat to human workers.

Drawing from my extensive background and expertise in AI ethics and advanced education, I can attest to the profound potential transformative impact of this technology. There is an allure to the ability to easily generate novel content such as text, images, and music with a few text-based prompts, but we must also remain acutely aware of the deeper ethical considerations at play. *"Its extraordinary ability to produce human-like writing, images, audio, and video have captured the world's imagination since the first generative AI*

---

[32] BER staff. (March 31, 2020). "Paying Attention: The Attention Economy". UC Berkely Economic Review. Available at *https://econreview.studentorg.berkeley.edu/paying-attention-the-attention-economy/*.

consumer chatbot was released to the public in the fall of 2022. ”[33]

What makes GenAI unique? With its ability to learn, adapt, and create, GenAI is not just another technology-based tool; it's a potentially radical shift in how we interact and create with technology.

The third wave of development is considered interactive AI.

AI vs. interactive AI vs generative AI

'Traditional' AI, interactive AI and generative AI share a number of common characteristics as well as a number of differences.

- **Common characteristics:** AI, interactive AI, and generative AI systems depend on large amounts of training data to function. Each learn patterns from the data and use that gained 'intelligence' to create output and to adapt to learned patterns. Additionally, each type of AI can be improved over time by adjusting their parameters based on feedback or new information.

- **Where they are different:** Traditional AI systems are usually created to perform a specific task or set of tasks more efficiently or at lower cost than a human worker. Interactive AI refers to AI that can react in conversation, in a human-like fashion, and interact with other systems. Generative AI is broader and the most talked about

---

[33] Pavlik, G. (September 15, 2023). What Is Generative AI (GenAI)? How Does It Work? Oracle Cloud Infrastructure Publications. Available at *https://www.oracle.com/artificial-intelligence/generative-ai/what-is-generative-ai/*.

today; it creates new and original content that reflects, but doesn't directly imitate, its training data. Traditional AI systems are trained primarily on data directly related to their intended function, while generative AI models are trained on larger, more diverse data sets. As a result, the training data for generative AI can be orders of magnitude larger than for traditional AI systems. Finally, traditional AI is almost always trained on labeled/categorized data using supervised learning techniques. At least initially, generative AI is trained, using unsupervised learning where data is unlabeled, and the AI software is given no explicit guidance.

Generative AI presents unique ethical challenges that may exceed those associated with traditional AI and even interactive AI. Before taking a quick look at some of the ethical challenges, we first must understand the foundation for generative AI systems.

How does it work?

In practice, no one knows exactly how generative AI does what it does – and that's the embarrassing truth. Theoretically, developers know how generative AI works because they have designed the various neural networks, iterating those designs to make them better and better. AI developers know exactly how the neurons are connected; they engineered each model's training process. And still *"We don't know how they do the actual creative task because what goes on inside the neural network layers is way too complex for us to decipher, at least today,"* said Dean Thompson.[34]

Generative AI is a large language model (LLM) that uses deep learning to analyze patterns in large sets of data and then imitates this to generate new content that appears human-generated. It does this by employing the neural networks previously discussed – a process that is loosely linked to the way the human brain processes, interprets, and learns from information over time.

To give an example, if you were to feed lots of artist creations into a generative AI model, it would eventually gain the ability to develop new images or art based on the content it's been trained on. This occurs because the machine-learning algorithms that power generative AI models learn from the information they're fed – in the case of art, this would include elements like color, design, scenery, etc.

But it is still a mystery exactly how a generative AI model arrives at an answer to a text prompt – whether it's an article, a piece of art, or a music score. This may be a controversial position, but more than a dozen researchers who were given early access to GPT-4 in Fall 2022 concluded that the intelligence with which it responded to the complex challenges they presented and the broad range of expertise it

---

[34] Dean Thompson is the former Chief Technology Officer (CTO) at various AI startups, such as LinkedIn and Yelp.

exhibited, provided solid evidence that GPT-4 had attained a form of general intelligence.[35]

The term 'generative AI' refers to a broad category of models based on an increasingly rich group of neural network variations.

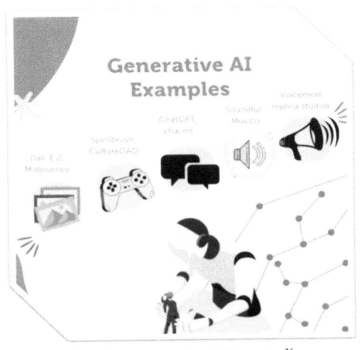

Figure 9: Generative AI Examples[36]

---

[35] Pavlik, G. (September 15, 2023). What is Generative AI (GenAI)? How Does It Work? Oracle Cloud Infrastructure Publications. Available at *https://www.oracle.com/artificial-intelligence/generative-ai/what-is-generative-ai/*.
[36] Fusemachines. Available at *https://insights.fusemachines.com/business-applications-of-chatgpt/*.

Types of generative AI models

A number of generative AI tools exist, although text models, such as ChatGPT, and image generation models like DALL-3 are perhaps the most well-known. As of March 2024, these are some of the most common generative AI models:

- **ChatGPT** – An AI language model developed by OpenAI that can answer questions and generate human-like responses from text prompts. Available at *https://openai.com/chatgpt.*

- **DALL-E 3** – Another OpenAI model that can create images and artwork from text prompts. Available at *https://openai.com/dall-e-3.*

- **Google Gemini** – Previously called Bard, Gemini is Google's answer to ChatGPT. It's trained on the PaLM large language model and can answer questions and generate text from prompts. Available at *https://gemini.google.com/?hl=en.*

- **Claude 2.1** – Anthropic's AI model offers a 200,000 token context window, which its creators claim can be used to brainstorm ideas, analyze images, and process longer text documents. Available at *https://www.anthropic.com/claude.*

- **Midjourney** – A product of the San Francisco-based research lab Midjourney Inc., this generative AI model interprets text prompts to produce images and artwork, similar to DALL-E. Available at *https://www.midjourney.com/home.*

- **Microsoft 365 Copilot** – Copilot for MS 365 integrates GPT into its Office 365 suite of applications. Users can use Copilot within Word, Excel, PowerPoint, and other applications to help them write more efficiently. Available at *https://copilot.microsoft.com/*.

- **GitHub Copilot** – An AI-powered coding tool that facilitates the process of coding applications by fixing common mistakes and suggesting lines of code. Available at *https://github.com/features/copilot*.
- **Llama 2** – An open-source large language model from Meta that can be used to create conversational AI models for chatbots and virtual assistants, similar to GPT-4. Available at *https://llama.meta.com/llama2/*.
- **Grok** – A new generative AI venture by Elon Musk, started in July 2023 after he left OpenAI, which he co-founded and helped fund. It is intended to serve as a robust research aid, helping users quickly access relevant information, process data, and develop new ideas. Available at *https://x.ai/*.

By the time you are reading this book, this list may have significantly expanded with new types of generative AI with advanced capabilities. The list, however, gives a good overview of the areas of creativity being influenced by generative AI.

Some benefits of generative AI

As a result of its 'intelligence,' generative AI theoretically has the potential to automate many routine and mundane tasks that make up much of the daily chores, allowing workers to focus on the higher-level parts of the job. We've only just begun to scratch the surface of potential uses for generative AI, and it is easy to see how organizations could potentially benefit by implementing it in their operations.

The table below shows some of the potential benefits of generative AI and the means by which these can be realized.

Table 1: Generative AI Benefits[37]

Generative AI Benefits	How Can These Be Achieved?		
	Knowledge Synthesis	Human–AI Collaboration	Speed
Increased Productivity	Organize and synthesize data, create drafts, facilitate research.	Educate users by providing new information, suggest new ways to address tasks and problems.	Accelerate learning and ability of the user to complete tasks.
Reduced Costs	Identify inefficiencies and redundancies.	Help users refine work processes, minimize human error.	Complete tasks more rapidly, reducing time to completion.
Improved Customer Satisfaction	Rapidly identify and retrieve customer information	Produce improved chatbots, human-level responses to queries, provide more data where human	Real-time updates and information to both customers and service reps.

---

[37] Adapted from Pavlik, G. (September 15, 2023). "What is Generative AI (GenAI)? How Does It Work?" Oracle Cloud Infrastructure Publications. Available at *https://www.oracle.com/artificial-intelligence/generative-ai/what-is-generative-ai/*.

	to facilitate resolution.	interaction is needed.	
Better-Informed Decision Making	Rapidly produce predictive analytics, scenario modeling, and risk assessments.	Provide detailed and customized recommendations and actionable strategies to decision makers.	Generate faster data retrieval and analysis than human counterparts.
Faster Product to Market	Create viable prototypes.	Test and troubleshoot prototypes and existing projects to identify areas of improvement.	Increase speed at which adjustments can be implemented.

As a result of these benefits, generative AI is of the most important strategic technology trends in decades. There are a wide variety of more specific applications in different industries and business functions, including the following:

- **Health care** – applications of generative AI include streamlined drug discovery and development, personalized medicine, improved medical imaging, and population/demographic-based health improvement.
- **Marketing and sales** – generative AI can prepare analyses of current market trends, consumer preferences, and historical sales data supporting product recommendations, inventory management, supply chain optimization, and virtual shopping assistants.

- **Education** – generative AI can have positive benefits, such as tutoring, personalized lesson development, and course design and content creation.

- **Banking** – generative AI can provide powerful tools for fraud prevention and detection, risk management, data privacy protection, and personalized loan review processes.

- **Customer service** – generative AI supports multiple languages, personalized customer engagement, rapid responses to customer queries, and tailored customer communications.

- **Manufacturing** – generative AI models can generate predictive models, allowing for improved maintenance and reduced downtime, quality control, production planning, and inventory management.

Other areas where generative AI shows potential benefit include fashion, human resources, code-based functions, gaming, travel, insurance, and support to lawyers.

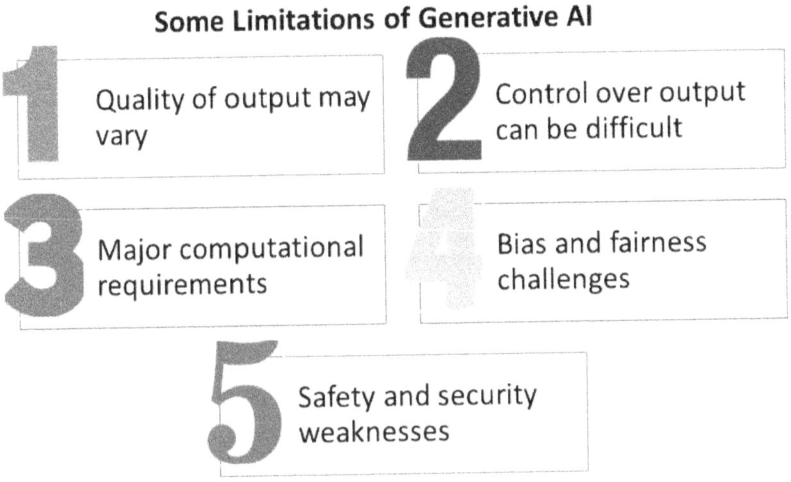

Some Limitations of Generative AI

Quality of output may vary

Control over output can be difficult

Major computational requirements

Bias and fairness challenges

Safety and security weaknesses

Figure 10: Some Limitations of Generative AI

But generative AI also has notable limitations. These include the following:

- **Quality of generated outputs:** Generative AI systems may not always produce high-quality outputs, and the generated outputs may contain errors or artifacts.

- **Control over the generated outputs:** It can be difficult to control the outputs generated by generative AI systems.

- **Computational requirements:** Generative AI requires specialized hardware and software, as well as skilled personnel to operate and maintain it.

- **Bias and fairness:** Generative AI systems can be biased and unfair.

- **Explainability and interpretability:** The exact way generative AI systems reach a particular conclusion or generate a specific output is not transparent.
- **Safety and security:** Generative AI systems can be vulnerable to attacks and can pose safety risks.

Societal and ethical concerns about the digital world and AI

"Prediction is difficult; especially about the future."[38]

Looking at the development of digital technologies, and that includes AI, it's easy to see the difficulty of evaluating the consequences of new technologies. When the cell phone was developed, who could have predicted that terrorists would use them to set off bombs? And when the Internet emerged, who saw that it would change everything from how we work to how we interact as a society?

Efforts are being made to evaluate the consequences and the related concerns associated with the increasing evolution of digital technologies and AI. This is especially important because of the wide use of AI technology. Any given AI algorithm could dramatically change the present, as well as the future, for people across the globe. Whereas other forms of technology might take time to develop, implement, and use on a large scale, with digital technology and AI you potentially have billions of people who are adapting and using this technology. Consequently, any small modification or output from the AI technology becomes instantly magnified. We neglect the necessity of applying ethics to

---

[38] This quote has been attributed to both Albert Einstein and Neils Bohr.

adjusting and course-correcting as digital and AI technologies are deployed.

The following graph illustrates how technology experts, academics, and lawmakers rated the level of concern in regard to AI:

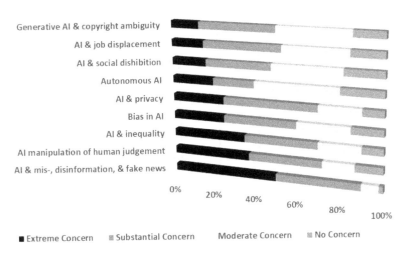

AI Areas of Concern

Figure 11: AI Areas of Concern[39]

Even the developers of AI and generative AI say there may be a 1 in 10 chance that AI could pose an existential threat to humanity. Whether they're right, some will say anyone developing AI capabilities is contributing to the problem.

---

[39] Derived from TechTrends 2024. InfoTech Research Group. Available as a downloadable .pdf at *https://www.infotech.com/research/ss/tech-trends-2024,*

The emergence of generative AI in particular has elicited extreme reactions on both sides of the risk spectrum. There are many who focus on the benefits. Others express their apprehension that increased reliance on the various types of AI and generative AI only brings us one step closer to human destruction. These are the extremes. Nevertheless, there are still important concerns that developers and organizations designing and implementing AI technologies need to understand and take steps to mitigate.

We'll take a deeper look at some of these concerns and others in the following chapters.

CHAPTER 4: THE ROLE OF AI AND GENERATIVE AI IN MISINFORMATION AND DISINFORMATION

> *"We are living in a post-truth era where perception is infinitely more important than the truth as far as society is concerned."*[40]
>
> **Ibrahim Altay**

One of the primary concerns regarding the use of AI and generative AI tools – particularly those accessible to the public – is their potential for spreading misinformation and/or disinformation and other harmful content. The impact could be extensive and severe, from perpetuating stereotypes, hate speech, and harmful ideologies to damaging personal and professional reputations.

What is misinformation, disinformation, and fake news?

These terms are often used interchangeably, but there are important differences.

---

[40] Altay, I. (May 28, 2018). "Pursuing facts in the post-truth era". Available at *https://www.dailysabah.com/readers-corner/2018/05/28/pursuing-facts-in-the-post-truth-era*.

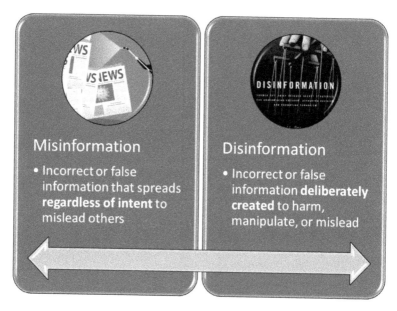

Figure 12: Misinformation vs Disinformation

Misinformation

Misinformation is – simply put – misleading or incorrect information that can spread without specific intent to do harm. Misinformation *"…is often used as an umbrella term to refer to many types of false information; more specifically it may refer to false information that is not shared to intentionally deceive or cause harm."*[41] Despite the lack of intent, the inadvertent or misguided sharing of misinformation can cause significant human, social, and political damage. Studies have shown that exposure to misinformation, especially prolonged exposure, can have a

---

[41] Wikipedia. Misinformation. Available at *https://en.wikipedia.org/wiki/Misinformation.*

lasting cognitive impact on how events are interpreted and remembered, even after the content has been corrected. In other words, once accepted, misinformation creates a bias that strongly resists revision.

In general, *"misinformation requires less cognitive effort for being processed and is more reliant on emotions than factual information: it is easier to read, and falsified content creators use a less diverse vocabulary, which may explain why misinformation is more prevalent among low-literacy individuals and more appealing to negative emotions and moral values, which may influence our ability to discern between misinformation and factual content."*[42]

There are many ways misinformation is generated and spread. One source of misinformation is when people share false information as a fact without thoroughly fact checking that information for accuracy. Research indicates that the ability to quickly share information online via AI-powered social media platforms has exacerbated the misinformation problem. A 2018 study of Twitter (now X) users by researchers at the Massachusetts Institute of Technology found that false information spreads more quickly than accurate information.[43] This gives credence to the rumored

---

[42] Carrasco-Farre, C. (2022). "The fingerprints of misinformation: how deceptive content differs from reliable sources in terms of cognitive effort and appeal to emotions". Available at *https://www.nature.com/articles/s41599-022-01174-9*.

[43] Vosoughi, S., et al. (March 9, 2018). "The spread of true and false news online". Science online. Available at *https://www.science.org/doi/10.1126/science.aap9559*.

statement by Churchill that *"A lie can travel halfway around the world while the truth is putting on its shoes."*

Other sources of misinformation include social media and even network news media. What, network news media? Aren't they intended to be the purveyors of truth? The answer lies in their need to attract readers and viewers. Social media platforms often cite 'freedom of speech' as a reason for allowing false information to continue on their platforms. *"Today, more than 8 in 10 Americans get their news on digital devices – beating out TV, radio or print. Among 18–29-year-olds, social media is the most common news source. They aren't the only ones turning to platforms for information; 53% of Americans get at least some of their news from social media. Twitter, Facebook, and TikTok have all become pseudo-news platforms."*[44] And what is presented to us on social media is determined by an AI algorithm, whose sole purpose is to keep the user online as long as possible. Sensationalized content tends to get users to spend more time on the platform and to get more shares. And the social media platforms prod users to share high-performing content further, so the algorithm ends up feeding other users and platforms with an ongoing flood of misinformation.

A number of ways to counteract misinformation have been considered, such as *"platform design changes, algorithmic changes, content moderation, de-platforming prominent actors that spread misinformation, and crowdsourcing*

---

[44] Micich, A. and Cross, R. J. (August 14, 2023). "How misinformation on social media has changed news". Available at *https://pirg.org/edfund/articles/misinformation-on-social-media/*.

misinformation detection or removing it. "[45] There is concern, however, that strong policy responses to misinformation could easily be used by government policymakers to strategically reduce freedom of speech, for example by silencing political opponents.

Disinformation

Disinformation differs from misinformation in that it is created with the intent to mislead – and therefore potentially more harmful. And unlike misinformation, the basis for disinformation is malicious and deceptive. It is generally shared initially with the goal of deceiving or misleading, even if those who subsequently share it do so innocently and unknowingly.

"Bad actors have leveraged this new information ecosystem by deliberately spreading disinformation to influence public opinion regarding vaccines, the COVID-19 pandemic, international affairs, political candidates, U.S. democracy, and other critical topics. These attempts at sowing distrust in our institutions have fueled vaccine hesitancy and skepticism, leading to major public health challenges. Disinformation has contributed to a rise of hate speech and political violence and initiated a revolving cycle of voter challenges and the introduction of voter suppression laws that have made it harder for voters—particularly older

---

[45] Altay, S., et al. (July 27, 2023). "A survey of expert views on misinformation: Definitions, determinants, solutions, and future of the field". Available at *https://misinforeview.hks.harvard.edu/article/a-survey-of-expert-views-on-misinformation-definitions-determinants-solutions-and-future-of-the-field/*.

voters, voters of color, and voters with disabilities—to participate in democracy. "[46]

Examples of potential uses of disinformation include:

- Governments or politicians using disinformation to manipulate public opinion and win elections
- Foreign agents facilitating disinformation campaigns to interfere in other countries' politics
- Businesses spreading disinformation about their products to mislead consumers
- Using propaganda as a form of disinformation to promote a specific ideology or agenda
- Military use of disinformation tactics to deceive enemies and gain an advantage in warfare
- Media spreading disinformation that reflects their political biases
- Using disinformation to create fear and panic among the public, leading to chaos and instability
- Creating disinformation to spread hate speech and incite violence

Disinformation can take many forms, such as fake news, propaganda, and conspiracy theories. It may also be shared in the form of manipulated images, videos, or audio clips, also known as deepfakes. Deepfakes and other advanced

---

[46] Palfrey, J. (March 14, 2014). "Misinformation and disinformation". Britannica online. Available at *https://www.britannica.com/topic/misinformation-and-disinformation.*

technologies have made disinformation even harder to detect and combat.

Deepfakes

Deepfakes are hyper-realistic digital imitation or falsification of images, video, and/or audio created by AI and neural networks using machine-learning models called generative adversarial networks (GANs). Although they tend to appear most often in pornography, deepfakes are contributing to the epidemic of misinformation and disinformation available via digital platforms.

It is one of the most interesting technologies developed over the past few years. And in many ways, it's also one of the scariest. You may have already seen images or videos of celebrities or well-known political figures appearing to say or do controversial things that they never actually said or did. While early deepfakes were fairly obvious to dismiss as being artificially fabricated, the latest generation of deepfake technology is blurring the lines between what's real and what's not.

How does a deepfake work?

Deepfakes operate by analyzing vast data sets of a target individual's images or recordings. The deep-learning model learns the intricacies of the target's facial expressions, voice patterns, and other distinctive features. Once trained, the model can generate highly realistic content that mimics the target's behavior or appearance.

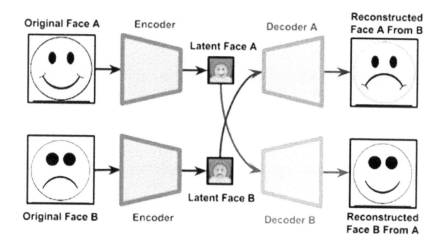

Figure 13: How a Deepfake Works

There are a number of tools to create deepfake images or videos that are readily available and relatively simple to use. These include the following free tools:

Table 2: Examples of Free Deepfake Tools

Product	Quality	Features	OS	User-friendliness
DeepFaceLab	One of the most popular and advanced free software. Allows users to create very realistic-looking content.	Advanced, powerful, and realistic-looking videos.	Windows, Linux, Mac OS.	Difficult to use, requires tutorials, steep learning curve.

MachineTube	Very easy to use. Has a lot of clips to play around with. Features an audio component that can modulate voices.	Moderate quality.	PC-based, compatible with any browser.	Very user-friendly, pre-made templates.
FaceSwap	Advanced deepfake maker. Good community support and tutorials available. Helps users learn how this type of technology works.	Open-source, support for Windows, Linux, MacOS, good community support for tutorials.	Windows, Linux, Mac OS.	Advanced, difficult to use but good for learning deepfake technology.

Are deepfakes dangerous?

Deepfakes have appeared in recent years showing politicians making claims that are the opposite of their actual position. One uploaded to a hacked Ukrainian news website depicted Volodymyr Zelensky, President of Ukraine, telling his soldiers to lay down their arms[47], or Barack Obama using profanity toward Donald Trump.[48] If such deceptions go viral, they could have an irreversible effect on world affairs.

One very real issue with deepfakes is their use of personal images without consent. Taylor Swift was one of the latest high-profile victims when deepfake pornographic images of her were proliferated across the social media platform X (formerly Twitter). Her status generated a widespread call for action and her image was quickly removed. That is often not the case for less well-known or unfortunate victims. In addition to its uses for pornography, some image-based deepfakes are used to humiliate or damage an individual's reputation. And for many, takedown and removal of deepfake images is a futile process. It is often an uphill battle, and there is no guarantee of its complete removal once it has been placed in the digital web.

Deepfakes allow filmmakers to create more diverse and imaginative content, such as inserting actors into roles they never played or adapting film endings to various creative visions. This resulted in one of the longest strikes in film industry history. Writers and actors were advocating for increased guardrails against their replacement through the use of AI and deepfake technology.

---

[47] Allyn, B. (March 16, 2022). "Deepfake video of Zelenskyy could be 'tip of the iceberg' in info war, experts warn". NPR online. Available at *https://www.npr.org/2022/03/16/1087062648/deepfake-video-zelenskyy-experts-war-manipulation-ukraine-russia.*
[48] Silverman, C. (April 17, 2018). "How To Spot A Deepfake Like The Barack Obama–Jordan Peele Video". BuzzFeed online. Available at *https://www.buzzfeed.com/craigsilverman/obama-jordan-peele-deepfake-video-debunk-buzzfeed.*

Another ethical concern is grounded in the potential of deepfakes to easily spread misinformation and disinformation. On an individual level, the ability to produce realistic images or videos of a person arguably poses serious risk in a justice system that relies on sight and observation to establish objective fact.

Further, deepfake images and videos risk advancing the development of echo chambers and epistemic bubbles where people may not know that these videos are fake. Therefore, they can be leveraged to champion or consolidate dangerous thinking. The ability of deepfakes to influence public opinion cannot be overstated. With today's technology, deepfakes can create convincingly false images or videos of public figures saying or doing things they never did, potentially manipulating public opinion and influencing election outcomes. The integrity of democratic processes in many nations could be directly threatened by the proliferation of deepfakes, as they undercut the foundational principle that free choice based on informed opinion forms the basis of democratic decision-making.

Earlier deepfakes were easier to detect. Technology, however, is advancing very quickly and the ability to detect a deepfake is increasingly unreliable. A recent study found that deepfake videos and images have become more believable and that people are more likely to engage with them.[49]

---

[49] Lee, J., & Shin, S. Y. (2022). "Something that they never said: multimodal disinformation and source vividness in understanding the power of AI-enabled deepfake news". Media Psychology, 25(4), 531-546.

Despite the very real concerns about the ethics of some forms of deepfakes, there are those who see positive value. *"Deepfake technology has been used to bring art to life, recreate the voices of historical figures, and to use celebrities' likeness to communicate powerful public health messages."*[50] For these reasons, deepfakes may also be able to help integrate AI into our lives in a more humanizing and personalized manner.

Even considering the benefits of deepfake technology, there is a definite need for stricter regulations, and people who abuse the scope of technology ought to be held accountable – if used for malicious purposes. Developers also bear responsibility for developing an app using deepfake technology that actively harms.

The image from Groundviews is helpful for thinking about the ecosystem of misinformation and disinformation, which can be organized into ten types.[51]

Detecting a deepfake

Deepfake technology is improving. It is increasingly difficult to recognize deepfakes created by various software. An alert eye, however, together with some knowledge minimizes their ability to fool. Here are a few things to look out for when trying to spot a deepfake:

---

[50] Goodwine, K. (December 7, 2020). "Ethical Considerations of Deepfakes". Available at *https://www.prindleinstitute.org/2020/12/ethical-considerations-of-deepfakes/.*
[51] Note that some sources say there are five types of misinformation, disinformation; and fake news; others lay claim to seven.

1. Unusual facial expressions and features

In most cases, the easiest way to identify a deepfake is to pay close attention to the eyes of the person in the image or video. Replicating things like eye movement and blinking is very difficult. The area around the mouth can also provide tell-tale indicators. A lot of deepfake tools may have good lip-syncing capability, but something will inevitably look odd after staring at the image or video for a while. Deepfaked individuals tend to have rather static – sometimes downright robotic – facial expressions and often look much more emotionless when compared to a regular person.

2. Blurring and coloring

A lot of deepfake videos and images really don't do a great job of matching one person's face to another person's body. That's why there will often be blurring or other strange effects surrounding the face, particularly near the hairline and neck. Another thing to watch for is color. Matching the exact same skin tone isn't easy. In some cases, it is easy to spot a deepfake video simply by looking for mismatched skin tones.

3. Audio cues

Deepfake technology is mainly used for manipulating images and video rather than audio. As a result, there are often video scenarios where person A has the face of person B, but the voice is still that of person A. Since technology is usually used to deepfake famous people, it's pretty easy to tell when something just doesn't sound right. As mentioned earlier, there are ways of replicating someone's voice, but these are far from perfect. Paying attention to audio characteristics like intonation, accent, or timbre can help identify a fake.

4. Tech help

Soon after deepfake software started to increase in popularity, several organizations began developing technology that could help spot deepfakes. In the case of a suspected deepfake video, Google's text-to-speech tool can help identify the original speaker. And researchers at universities and agencies, such as DARPA[52], are working on technology that can automatically spot deepfakes.

Types of misinformation, disinformation, and fake news

Groundviews[53] developed the following graphic, which identifies ten types of misinformation, disinformation, and fake news:

---

[52] DARPA is the Defense Advanced Research Projects Agency for the US, with a mission to develop breakthrough technologies focused on national security requirements.
[53] Groundviews is a citizens journalism website that highlights alternative perspectives on governance, human rights, the arts and literature, peace-building, and other issues.

Figure 14: 10 Types of Mis- and Disinformation[54]

---

[54] Image courtesy of Groundviews via Creative Commons. Available at *https://groundviews.org/2018/05/12/infographic-10-types-of-mis-and-disinformation/.*

The role played by AI in misinformation, disinformation, and deepfakes

"The ability to deceive from AI has put the problem of mis- and disinformation on steroids," said Lisa Gilbert of Public Citizen.[55]

AI-based systems are playing an important role in the dangerous spread of misinformation, disinformation, and deepfakes. They do this not only by providing the means to generate false content but also by facilitating the dissemination of false or incorrect information to a targeted audience and at an enormous scale. *"At least 47 governments deployed commentators to manipulate online discussions in their favor during the coverage period, double the number from a decade ago. Meanwhile, AI-based tools that can generate text, audio, and imagery have quickly grown more sophisticated, accessible, and easy to use, spurring a concerning escalation of these disinformation tactics. Over the past year, the new technology was utilized in at least 16 countries to sow doubt, smear opponents, or influence public debate."*[56]

Targeted content methods using AI-based systems were initially developed to enable advertisements directed at specific consumers for the sake of efficiency. AI algorithms record every action we take online (which can be active or passive) to present content that will increase the time we

---

[55] Lisa Gilbert is the CEO of Public Citizen, which advocates for federal and state regulation of AI's use in politics.

[56] Funk, A., et al. (October 2023). "The Repressive Power of Artificial Intelligence". Freedom House online. Available at *https://freedomhouse.org/report/freedom-net/2023/repressive-power-artificial-intelligence.*

spend using the online platform. This same algorithmic design based on micro-targeting can also directly intensify the propagation of both mis- and disinformation.

Digital doppelgängers – a mirror image of you

Imagine for just a moment a clone or human avatar that looks, talks, and behaves just like you, created by AI with the ability to reflect your speech, your appearance, and your mannerisms with eerie precision. This is totally possible due to the advances in AI deep-learning technologies such as interactive deepfake applications, voice conversion, and virtual actors. It's now possible to digitally replicate a person's appearance and behavior and create a digital clone or avatar.

A 2023 study looked at the potential societal and psychological effects of AI clones. It found significant ethical implications, such as: *"(1. doppelgänger-phobia) the abusive potential of AI clones to exploit and displace the identity of an individual elicits negative emotional reactions; (2. identity fragmentation) creating replicas of a living individual threatens their cohesive self-perception and unique individuality; and (3. living memories) interacting with a clone of someone with whom the user has an existing relationship poses risks of misrepresenting the individual or developing over-attachment to the clone."*[57]

---

[57] Lee, P., et al. (April 16, 2023). "Speculating on Risks of AI Clones to Selfhood and Relationships: Doppelganger-phobia, Identity Fragmentation, and Living Memories". Available at https://dl.acm.org/doi/10.1145/3579524.

Could you be replaced by your digital clone or avatar?

The short answer – possibly. These clones or avatars are incredibly realistic and can almost undetectably mimic the original human, as indicated in the photo below. This photo was extracted from a YouTube presentation featuring a real news reporter, Tom Mackenzie, and his digital clone. I recommend watching the video at *https://www.bloomberg.com/news/videos/2023-06-02/human-avatars-your-ai-powered-digital-twin*.

Should we fear that our jobs or even our persona will be taken over by such an avatar? Well, when Mackenzie asked his avatar that question, his avatar assured him that at least when it comes to his job as a journalist, it's safe – for now!

Figure 15: The Real Mackenzie[58]

---

[58] Molenaar, K. (October 7, 2024). Discover the Top 12 Virtual Influencers for 2024 – Listed and Ranked. Available at https://influencermarketinghub.com/virtual-influencers/

The digital clone/avatar market is growing fast, expected to exceed $525 billion by the end of the decade.

Digital influencers

Some organizations are using digital avatars as virtual influencers. These virtual influencers are entirely computer-generated characters designed to interact with audiences in a human-like manner. While we probably won't be seeing human influencers replaced by AI-generated avatars just yet, at the rate it's going, virtual influencers may become as popular – if not more popular – than traditional influencers.

Christopher Travers, the founder of VirtualHumans.org, argues that virtual influencers can do anything that human influencers can do, but with more control and engagement – and for less cost. Due to advances in the AI used in creating digital humans/avatars, the differences in appearance between human-looking virtual influencers and real influencers are becoming harder to identify.

Here are a few of the more well-known and popular virtual influencers.[59] As you can see, it is almost impossible to distinguish these virtual creations from real human beings.

---

[59] A full list of the top 12 virtual influencers can be found at https://influencermarketinghub.com/virtual-influencers/.

Lu do Magalu

A Brazilian-'born' digital influencer with more than 14 million followers on Facebook alone. Her avatar has been used by brands like Red Bull, Samsung, and most popularly, by the magazine Luiza.

Figure 16: Lu do Magalu, Brazilian Digital Influencer[60]

Miquela Sousa

Commonly known as Lil Miquela, is the first virtual influencer and is best known as a virtual model for brands like Prada, Dior, and others. She's also appeared as a singer who produced a music video called "Hard Feelings." In

---

[60] Molenaar, K. (October 7, 2024). Discover the Top 12 Virtual Influencers for 2024 – Listed and Ranked. Available at *https://influencermarketinghub.com/virtual-influencers/*.

2018, Time Magazine named her one of the 25 most influential people on the Internet – although Miquela isn't a real person.[61]

Figure 17: Lil Miquela, Virtual Avatar for Designer Brands[62]

---

[61] Time Magazine. (June 30, 2018). "The 25 Most Influential People on the Internet". Available at *https://time.com/5324130/most-influential-internet/*.

[62] Molenaar, K. (October 7, 2024). Discover the Top 12 Virtual Influencers for 2024 – Listed and Ranked. Available at *https://influencermarketinghub.com/virtual-influencers/*.

Shudu

Hailed as the world's first digital supermodel. Shudu has modeled for Balmain and appeared on the cover of Vogue magazine. Her appearance was based on iconic models such as Naomi Campbell and Grace Jones.

Figure 18: Shudu, Virtual Avatar Based on Iconic Models[63]

The appearance and mannerisms of each of these digital avatars were carefully curated to appeal to a specific audience or demographic.

There are significant ethical implications associated with both digital clones and virtual influencers. As digital clones become increasingly difficult to distinguish from their human original, real humans may be co-opted by the clone and could easily be used to further misinformation and disinformation. The potential to create digital clones without

---

[63] *https://influencermarketinghub.com/virtual-influencers/*.

the specific knowledge or consent of the original person also raises the specter of a new kind of 'AI replica identity theft' or 'AI personality theft.'

Others fall victim to the promise of digital immortality and securing a digital legacy as an incentive to create a digital AI replica of themselves.

Virtual influencers are specifically designed to be 'perfect' and have the potential to perpetuate unrealistic life and physical appearance standards. Their extremely realistic appearance gives them a credibility that is not real or earned through life experience. Given that virtual influencers are controlled by their creators, there is a risk of spreading misinformation or exhibiting bias toward certain demographics, especially if their artificial nature is not disclosed clearly.

What are the potential ethical implications of the increase in misinformation, disinformation, and deepfakes?

If someone embraces the idea that mankind has never touched the moon, that a mass shooting was a hoax, or there was no pandemic, are they not just incorrect, but ethically wrong?

Governments, political actors, and organizations across the globe in both democracies and tyrannies are leveraging AI to generate text, images, and videos designed to manipulate public opinion in their favor and to automatically censor any critical digital content. On an annual basis, Freedom on the Net scores and ranks countries according to their relative degree of Internet freedom, measured by a number of factors such as Internet shutdowns, laws limiting online expression, censorship of dissenting or 'unpopular' opinions, and retaliation for online speech. The 2024 report released in October determined that global Internet freedom declined for the fourteenth consecutive year, driven in part by the proliferation of AI and generative AI.[64]

The use of falsified information, such as fake news, to influence human decision making is not new. Misinformation, disinformation, and fake news have long been present in human communication. And newsmakers and politicians have long known that sensationalism sells well. Around 31 BC, the Roman *"Octavian waged a propaganda campaign against Antony that was designed to smear his reputation. This took the form of 'short, sharp slogans written upon coins in the style of archaic Tweets.' These slogans painted Antony as a womanizer and a drunk, implying he had become Cleopatra's puppet, having been corrupted by his affair with her. Octavian became Augustus, the first Roman Emperor and 'fake news had allowed Octavian to hack the republican system once and for all'."*[65] It worked because Octavian, and not Antony, became the first Roman emperor bearing the name Augustus Caesar.

The pervasiveness of false information on digital platforms drastically weakens an individual's capacity to make free

---

[64] Funk, A., et al. (October 2024). "The Struggle for Trust Online". Freedom House online. Available at *https://freedomhouse.org/report/freedom-net/2024/struggle-trust-online.*
[65] Posetti, J. and Matthews, A. (July 2018). "A 'short guide' to the history of fake news and disinformation". Available at *https://www.icfj.org/sites/default/files/2018-07/A%20Short%20Guide%20to%20History%20of%20Fake%20News%20and%20Disinformation_ICFJ%20Final.pdf.*

and informed decisions, which is an essential prerequisite for autonomy – or the ability to live life according to one's own decisions and not as a product of distorted or manipulative external entities. Alongside misinformation and disinformation, echo chambers can become a threat to independent thinking and the democratic process. An echo chamber can be defined as *"an environment in which individuals encounter only beliefs or opinions that coincide with their own, so that their existing views are reinforced and alternative ideas are not considered."*[66]

Today, AI-generated content creates an increasing set of challenges in distinguishing reality from fabricated content being fed to consumers via AI algorithms, which can be exploited to generate political chaos or manipulate public opinion, eroding public trust in established institutions and spreading societal discord. *"As AI-generated content on the internet becomes normalized, "it's going to allow for political actors to cast doubt about reliable information. It's a phenomenon known as "liar's dividend," in which wariness of fabrication makes people more skeptical of true information, particularly in times of crisis or political conflict when false information can run rampant."*[67]

---

[66] Bergamini, D. (September 23, 2020). "Need for democratic governance of Artificial Intelligence". Committee on Political Affairs and Democracy – Council of Europe. Available at *https://assembly.coe.int/LifeRay/POL/Pdf/TextesProvisoires/2020/2020 0908-DemocraticAI-EN.pdf.*

[67] Ryan-Mosesly, T. (October 4, 2023). How generative AI is boosting the spread of disinformation and propaganda. MIT Review online. Available at *https://www.technologyreview.com/2023/10/04/1080801/generative-ai-boosting-disinformation-and-propaganda-freedom-house/.*

Examples of AI-generated misinformation, disinformation, and deepfakes

There are many recent examples of how AI technology can be used to create and distribute misinformation, disinformation, and fake news. In the US in early 2024, robocalls impersonating President Joe Biden urged voters in New Hampshire to abstain from voting in January's primary election. The calls were later traced to a political consultant who said he was trying to publicize the dangers of AI deepfakes.[68]

In India, AI versions of dead politicians have been brought back to compliment elected officials, according to Al Jazeera.[69]

---

[68] Ramer, H. (February 26, 2024). "Political consultant behind fake Biden robocalls says he was trying to highlight a need for AI rules". Available at *https://apnews.com/article/ai-robocall-biden-new-hampshire-primary-2024-f94aa2d7f835ccc3cc254a90cd481a99.*

[69] Christopher, N. (February 12, 2024). "How AI is resurrecting dead Indian politicians as election looms". Available at *https://www.aljazeera.com/economy/2024/2/12/how-ai-is-used-to-resurrect-dead-indian-politicians-as-elections-loom?utm_source=substack&utm_medium=email.*

4: The role of AI and generative AI in misinformation and disinformation

Figure 19: AI-generated Video of M Karunanidhi, Deceased Indian Politician[70]

Fact checkers from Full Fact identified at least eight examples of how AI was used to create fake news. One of these was an image that appeared to show a reconciliation of Prince Willliam and Prince Harry at the King's Coronation. It was fake. And later was revealed to have been generated using the Midjourney image generator.

---

[70] Christopher, 2024.

Figure 20: Fake Image of Prince William and Prince Harry Reconciliation[71]

Even before former President Trump posted his real mug shot on X (formerly Twitter), generative AI technologies were used to create a fake image that went viral, with more than a million views in a very short period.

All of these could have significant impacts on social and political realities.

Manipulation of reality and the proliferation of fake content can have severe economic impacts as well. For example, false information about organizations or markets can lead to stock market manipulation and economic instability.

---

[71] Nanan-Sen, S. (2024). Prince William and Prince Harry's teary-eyed reunion goes viral as AI image racks up thousands of likes. Available at *https://www.msn.com/en-us/lifestyle/lifestyle-buzz/prince-william-and-prince-harrys-teary-eyed-reunion-goes-viral-as-ai-image-racks-up-thousands-of-likes/ar-AA1lriDL.*

One notable example occurred more than a decade ago. In 2010, *"...the U.S. Stock market experienced a sudden and severe drop, with the Dow Jones Industrial average plummeting by nearly 1,000 points in a matter of minutes. This crash was triggered by a series of algorithmic trades executed by an AI-driven trading system, which inadvertently set off a chain reaction of automated selling. The incident highlighted the vulnerability of financial markets to rapid and uncontrolled AI-driven trading, leading to renewed calls for stricter regulations."*[72]

Will generative AI make it easier to create and spread mis- and disinformation?

Many leading AI researchers, scientists, and lawmakers are concerned that generative AI will make it even easier to create realistic but false or misleading content to a much greater degree, with potentially catastrophic consequences for individual and societal behavior, the public information sphere, and even for democracy. The Harvard Kennedy School places these concerns into four categories[73]:

---

[72] "Artificial Intelligence and Price Manipulation: A New Era of Market Abuse". (March 10, 2024). Available at
https://fastercapital.com/content/Artificial-Intelligence-and-Price-Manipulation--A-New-Era-of-Market-Abuse.html.

[73] Simon, F., et al. (October 18, 2023). "Misinformation reloaded? Fears about the impact of generative AI on misinformation are overblown". Available at
https://misinforeview.hks.harvard.edu/article/misinformation-reloaded-fears-about-the-impact-of-generative-ai-on-misinformation-are-overblown/.

Table 3: Concerns Related to Generative AI

Generative AI Concerns according to Harvard Kennedy School		
Generative AI Concern	**Explanation**	**Potential Consequence**
Increased quantity of mis-, disinformation and deepfakes	Due to the ease of access and use, generative AIs can be used to create mis-/disinformation at scale at little to no cost to individuals and organized actors	Increased amount of mis-, disinformation and/or deepfakes allows ill-intentioned actors to "flood the zone" with incorrect or misleading information, thus drowning out factual content and/or sowing discord
Increased quality of mis-, disinformation and deepfakes	Due to the technical capabilities and ease of use, generative AIs can be used to create higher-quality mis-, disinformation and deepfakes	Increased quality of mis-, disinformation and deepfakes can lead to increased persuasive potential, creating content that is more believable and harder to verify. This would either allow for the spread of false information or contribute to a general loss of trust in all types of news
Increased personalization of mis-, disinformation and deepfakes	Due to the technical capabilities and ease of use, generative AIs can easily be used to create high-quality mis-, disinformation or deepfakes personalized to a user's preferences	Greater influence on users of mis-, disinformation and fake news with the same outcome as above
Involuntary generation of plausible but false information	Generative AIs can generate useful content (e.g., code generation). However, they can also generate plausible-seeming information that is also entirely inaccurate. Without intending to, users could thus generate misinformation, which could potentially spread.	Misinforming users of generative AI and digital platforms and those with whom the information may be shared

And today, by means of free and low-cost generative AI from companies like Google and OpenAI, just about anyone can create high-quality deepfakes or other forms of disinformation and misinformation with just a simple text prompt. This is the first technology to have impact in a realm that was previously reserved for humans: the autonomous production of content in text, media, or visual form using a human-like understanding of language and meaning.

And this is precisely what links generative AI to the dangers of misinformation and disinformation – it is often impossible to differentiate content originating from a human or a machine. So, can we really trust what we hear, see, or read in today's digital world?

Strategies for identifying and combatting mis-, disinformation and fake news/deepfakes

Mis-, disinformation, and fake news are not new concepts, but the rate at which they can spread is – especially as the result of AI algorithms on online platforms. Many users of these platforms find it challenging to sort real news from fake news.

Here are ten valuable strategies and tips for recognizing misinformation, disinformation, and fake news:

1. **Conduct a visual assessment:** Online platforms and content presenting misinformation, disinformation, or fake news often look amateurish, present a lot of annoying ads, and use altered images or videos.
2. **Check the source of the information:** Determine if the source is considered reputable, such as the Wall Street Journal, BBC, or Forbes. If the content cites an unknown

source, do more research. For example, if a story looks like it is from the US Centers for Disease Control and Prevention (CDC), go to the CDC's own website to verify the information.

3. **Identify the author:** Stories that contain misinformation, disinformation, or fake news may not specify an author. Check the author for credibility by searching them online for other articles. Look at the profile photo – if the image doesn't appear to be original, it's likely that the content is fake.

4. **Identify the message:** Misinformation, disinformation, and fake news will often use sensational headlines as clickbait, may have an angry tone, or make outrageous assertions.

5. **Assess spelling, grammar, and punctuation:** If a story has a lot of CAPS, poor grammar or spelling, and lots of exclamation points, it's probably unreliable.

6. **Check the web domain:** Many fake stories often have URLs that look odd, such as nbc.com.co, to mimic legitimate news sources.

7. **Look out for sponsored content:** Examine the page for such labels as 'paid sponsor' or 'advertisement.' The associated articles frequently bait readers into buying something, whether they are legitimate or deceitful. Some of these ads may also take users to malicious sites to install malware.

8. **Determine if it's parody or satire:** There are many legitimate websites that post satire or parody of real news. Check the website to see if they consistently post

satirical stories or if they are known for satire. One such site is *The Onion* at *https://www.theonion.com/*.

9. **Check other reliable sources:** Search other reputable news sites and media outlets to see if they are reporting on the same story. Legitimate media outlets have qualified fact checkers to verify the legitimacy of the story (even if they aren't always accurate either!).

10. **Use fact checkers:** Fact-checkers are an important source of help to identify if a news story is credible. These sites conduct independent reviews and research to determine the accuracy of the information by checking multiple reputable media sources. Popular fact-checking sites include:

   - FactCheck.org (*https://www.factcheck.org/*)
   - Snopes.com (*https://www.snopes.com/*)
   - PolitiFact.com (*https://www.politifact.com/*)
   - BBC Verify
     (*https://www.bbc.com/news/reality_check*)

In addition to strategies to address misinformation and disinformation, Marlynn Wei in Psychology Today proposed specific recommendations for ensuring the ethical use of digital clones/avatars. These are presented in full here:

1. The use of a person's likeness, identity, and personality, including AI replicas, should be under the control of the person themselves or a designated decision maker who has been assigned that right. Those who are interested in creating their own AI replica should be given the right to remain in control of and be able to monitor and

control its activity. If the person is no longer alive, then the right should be passed to whoever is in charge of their digital estate.

2. AI replicas (e.g., chatbots, avatars, and digital twins) should be considered a digital extension of one's identity and self and thus afforded similar protections and sense of respect. AI replicas can change one's self-perception, identity, online behavior, or one's sense of self. The Proteus effect describes how the depiction of an avatar will change its behavior in virtual worlds and likely applies to AI replicas.

3. AI replicas should disclose to users that they are AI and offer people a chance [to] opt out of interaction with them. This is an important feature for the trustworthiness of AI replicas in general. For AI replicas of those who are no longer living, these interactions could impact family members and loved ones psychologically and potentially interfere with grieving.

4. AI replicas come with risks, including risk of misuse and reputational costs, so informed consent to create, share, and use AI replicas should be required. Empirical research on deepfakes suggests that representations of a person, even if not real, will still influence people's attitudes about the person and potentially even plant false memories of that person in others. A new research study on AI clones found that people express fears of doppelgänger-phobia, identity fragmentation and false memories. Users should be informed of these risks. One

researcher has proposed Digital Do Not Reanimate (DDNR) orders.

5. Creating and sharing an AI replica without the person's permission may lead to harmful psychological effects to the portrayed person, similar to identity theft or deepfake misuse. Consent from the portrayed person, or their representative, is essential. Having a digital version of oneself made and used without one's permission could lead to psychological stress similar to the well-established negative emotional impacts of identity theft and deepfakes. People whose identities are used without their permission can experience fear, stress, anxiety, helplessness, self-blame, vulnerability, and feeling violated.[74]

---

[74] Wei, Marlynn. (January 9, 2024). "New Psychological and Ethical Dangers of 'AI Identity Theft'". Psychology Today. Available at *https://www.psychologytoday.com/gb/blog/urban-survival/202401/new-psychological-and-ethical-dangers-of-ai-identity-theft.*

CHAPTER 5: AI AND ONLINE DISINHIBITION

> *"Cyberspace offers independence and freedom to be the way one wants to be – benignly honest with the best of intentions or toxically mean without having any self-reflective awareness as to why..."*[75]
>
> **John Suler**

Have you ever thought about what makes people ruder or meaner on the Internet? Why do some individuals express aggressive remarks, harshly criticize opinions, and fight over comments? Or so freely share sensitive traumatic experiences on public forums? Why do people do things online that they probably wouldn't do in person? The answer lies in what is termed the 'online disinhibition effect.'

Research on behavior in a digital online environment refers to disinhibition as impulsive–compulsive behavior, such as engaging in risky behavior, gambling, bullying, and posting inappropriate or sensationalized content. It is generally believed that the combination of invisibility and anonymity is the primary contributor to disinhibition.

---

[75] Suler, J. (May 10, 2016). "The Online Disinhibition Effect, 20 Years Later". Cambridge University Press. Available at *https://www.cambridgeblog.org/2016/05/the-online-disinhibition-effect-20-years-later/.*

Figure 21: Online Disinhibition Effect[76]

Individuals can create an online persona that can say just about anything without fear of repercussions or restriction in ways that they would not ordinarily be able to do or say in a traditional, offline situation. The online persona can allow people to experiment and express themselves in ways that might be considered socially inappropriate in the analog world. This can be due to the anonymity provided by online platforms, the lack of direct consequences for actions, and the absence of social cues[77] in digital communication.

Two types of online disinhibition have been identified:

---

[76] Shutterstock/AlexanderPavlov.
https://www.govtech.com/policy/drawing-a-line-between-internet-trolls-and-the-first-amendment.html.
[77] Social cues are ways humans use to communicate without words or in addition to verbal communication. These cues can be used to display our emotions or mindsets by using our facial expressions, physical posture, and/or verbal messaging.

- **Benign disinhibition** – is essentially self-disclosure. This is particularly evident in adolescents since *"...the online environment is characterized by fewer inhibitions and behavioral boundaries, self-disclosure occurs sooner and is often more intimate than it would be in similar, first-time face-to-face (FtF) encounters."*[78]

- **Toxic disinhibition** – in this case, disinhibition can turn 'ugly' and individuals may act more rudely, aggressively, or angry online. Typical examples of toxic disinhibition include cyber bullying and flaming, which is an aggressive online outburst.

What are some of the most common sources of online disinhibition?

John Suler, PhD, identified several factors that are common sources of both benign and toxic disinhibition:

- **Dissociative anonymity** – online identity becomes compartmentalized into an 'online self,' which is regarded as invisible and anonymous, and an 'offline self,' which is perceived as different and physically distinct. Individuals may think of the online self as not being real since the digital environment seems so virtual and without boundaries. Once dissociated from reality, morals, ethics, and norms can change as well. It is much easier for individuals to reject responsibility for negative

---

[78] Davis, K. (2012). "Friendship 2.0: Adolescents' experiences of belonging and self-disclosure online". *Journal of Adolescence, 35,* 1527-1536. *http://dx.doi.org/10.1016/j.adolescence.2012.02.013.*

actions and not acknowledge responsibility by denying actions, using smoke screens, or diverting the blame.

- **Invisibility** – an individual can communicate with or about others online without significant worry about how you appear to them. People tend to feel more gutsy, less scared, and more motivated to take risks.

- **Asynchronicity** – many online digital conversations occur asynchronously without the individual being required to respond immediately. When we opt out of the immediate conversation, it can disinhibit us because it disconnects us from the conversational feedback loop.

- **Solipsistic introjection** – the absence of face-to-face cues and real-time feedback between individuals can lead to vague self-boundaries. In some ways, other people on the online platforms become a part of your shared mind. Introjection occurs when others' thoughts feel like your own thoughts and opinions.

- **Dissociative imagination** – some individuals carefully draw the boundary between their online personas and their offline selves. So, for instance, the online persona as a sorcerer might disappear the moment that person is no longer involved in online role-playing. The self that lives in the digital world separates into its own domain of existence.

- **Minimization of status and authority** – online, the playing field seems more level, which reduces authority disparities and makes it simple to send an offensive or caustic email or post content that would never have been said in person. Status and social class are more ambiguous, and social hierarchies based on age, experience, respect, fame, expertise, etc. tend to mean less.[79]

Does AI increase the emergence of online disinhibition?

AI in its various forms has the potential to increase the phenomena of online disinhibition.

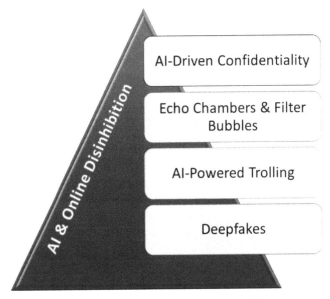

Figure 22: AI and Online Disinhibition

Here are a few examples of how this can happen:

---

[79] Suler, J. (2004). "The Online Disinhibition Effect". Cyberpsychology & behavior, Vol. 7, No. 3. Available at *https://www.researchgate.net/publication/8451443_The_Online_Disinhibition_Effect*.

- **AI-driven confidentiality** – AI can help individuals mask their true identities or construct sophisticated online personas. As a result, they feel less responsible for their activities and believe they can behave without consequences – the increased anonymity can then lead to increased disinhibition. The capacity to hide behind AI-generated avatars or chatbots may also intensify disinhibited behavior by reducing the perceived danger of exposure or retaliation.

- **Echo chambers and filter bubbles** – echo chambers and filter bubbles are often conflated, but there are subtle differences. In both cases, AI algorithms shape the online experience by curating content based on identified user partiality and common behavior. This can lead to situations in which users are largely exposed to information and opinions that reinforce existing belief sets. Disinhibition can grow in these contexts as people feel validated and reinforced by like-minded others, leading to more severe and polarizing expressions of their ideas.

- **Trolling and harassment powered by AI** – advanced AI technologies can be used to automate and intensify trolling and abuse. Chatbots or AI- powered tools can be configured to develop and disseminate inappropriate or destructive content on a massive scale, aimed at specific persons or communities. Because AI-driven harassment is automated and anonymous, it can have a greater impact on victims and make it difficult to address or combat such behavior effectively.

- **Deepfake technology** – deepfake technology based on AI permits the development of incredibly realistic fake images, movies, or audio recordings that can fool and manipulate others. This technology has the potential to be abused to disseminate false information, manufacture evidence, or harm someone's reputation.

What are the possible implications of disinhibition?

Disinhibition can have a wide variety of effects, both for the individual demonstrating it, those who are the victims, and even for the larger online community.

- **Negative interpersonal interactions** – in online contacts, disinhibition can lead to increased violence, antagonism, and conflict. Cyber bullying, trolling, or harassment can cause emotional anguish and injury to others. This can lead to broken relationships, poisonous online groups, and people feeling unsafe or unwilling to participate in online discussions.

- **Harmed reputation** – online disinhibition can lead to people sharing unsuitable or offensive content without thinking about the long-term effects. Such activities can harm their reputation, both in online and real communities. Online behavior can have real-life consequences in the digital era, influencing work opportunities, relationships, and social standing.

- **Legal ramifications** – in extreme circumstances, uninhibited online behavior can exceed legal lines. Threats, hate speech, defamation, or the dissemination of illegal content can all result in legal repercussions, such as fines or even criminal charges. The sense of anonymity online can occasionally drive people to participate in behaviors they would never consider in person, unaware of the potential legal consequences.

- **Emotional and psychological consequences** – disinhibition can have a negative impact on the individual who exhibits it. Engaging in violent or offensive online behavior can set off a negative loop that leads to increasing stress, guilt, or remorse. Excessive online disinhibition may also contribute to the blurring of boundaries between your online and offline identities, perhaps leading to identity confusion or the loss of true self-expression.

- **Social isolation and exclusion** – disinhibited behavior can lead to social isolation, as others may distance themselves from persons who habitually engage in hostile or abusive online behavior. Individuals may be prohibited or restricted from participating in online communities if rules or consequences are enforced to prevent disinhibited behavior.

Strategies for addressing toxic online disinhibition

Benign disinhibition is often encouraged and can have positive and pro-social results. Toxic disinhibition, on the other hand, causes offense, in general, and emotional harm, in particular. Angry, misanthropic, racist, and threatening online actions are often a result of toxic disinhibition, with often highly toxic results.

For this reason, it's important to look at strategies, or actions that can be taken, to minimize toxic online disinhibition while fostering the positive elements of benign disinhibition. These strategies can be applied in both educational and workplace environments or by online platforms themselves:

1. Encourage face-to-face encounters, whether online or in person. Individuals are less likely to display negative behaviors in an in-person environment or when in-person communications are replicated.

2. Reduce asynchronicity by making communication synchronous, and therefore more visible and less anonymous, to lessen unpleasant, angry, or harmful communications.

3. Foster 'netiquette' by mitigating the disassociation that has become the norm in some online behavior.

4. Develop and enforce a code of behavior that prohibits racist, sexist, homophobic, divisive language, profanity, and harassment in all its forms.

CHAPTER 6: BIASED BRAINS – CHALLENGING ALL TYPES OF BIAS

> *"The growing use of artificial intelligence in sensitive areas, including for hiring, criminal justice, and healthcare, has stirred a debate about bias and fairness. Yet human decision making in these and other domains can also be flawed, shaped by individual and societal biases that are often unconscious. Will AI's decisions be less biased than human ones? Or will AI make these problems worse?"*[80]
>
> **Jake Silberg and James Manyika**

What is AI bias? AI or machine-learning bias, also known as algorithm bias, refers to the tendency of AI algorithms to reflect human biases in the training data. It is a phenomenon that occurs when an algorithm delivers – usually unintentionally – systematically biased results as a consequence of erroneous assumptions of the AI process.

How does AI bias occur?

AI and generative models mirror the data they're fed. If an AI model is trained on or ingests biased data, ranging from

---

[80] Silberg, J. and Manyika, J. (June 6, 2019). Tackling bias in artificial intelligence (and in humans). Available at *https://www.mckinsey.com/featured-insights/artificial-intelligence/tackling-bias-in-artificial-intelligence-and-in-humans.*

gaps in perspectives to harmful and prejudicial content, bias could be manifested in its output. Consider facial recognition software, which, when biased, might wrongly identify individuals, leading to potential legal confrontations or public relations disasters. Or if an organization has historically been somewhat homogenous, the AI model may cross-reference new applicants with the 'ideal' hire and eliminate qualified candidates just because they don't fit the mold even if the organization is not intentionally perpetuating those hiring practices.

If the data used to train the algorithm is more characteristic of some groups of people than others, the output from the AI may also be worse for unrepresented or under-representative demographic groups. In recruiting, for example, AI used to review job applications relies on the organization's historical data to make selections for IT professionals. But historically, most IT staff have been male, so the AI algorithm in the application review system might display a bias toward male applicants.

Bias can also happen based on the conscious or unconscious prejudices on the part of developers, or it can occur as a result of undetected errors in the training data.

Some developers refer to the phenomenon of AI bias as a 'magical black box.' This really means that even the developers don't always fully understand how AI generates biased content. The AI can be trained on input data to create output, but the system's code or the logic that produced the output cannot be examined or explained.

There are reasons for the black box in AI. In many cases, an AI or the algorithm itself may be hidden so to protect intellectual property, AI developers may put the model in a black box. Another approach software developers take to protect the AI model is to obscure the data used to train the model – in other words, also put the training data in a black box.

Developers are working on creating more explainable AI, in essence to create a 'glass box.' But often driven by profit motives and IP protections initiatives, many developers may be reluctant to fully expose their AI models. However, this is changing. In May 2024, a team of researchers at the AI company Anthropic[81] announced a breakthrough in opening the AI 'black box.' The researchers examined one of Anthropic's AI models – Claude 3 Sonnet, a version of the company's Claude 3 language model – *"and used a technique known as 'dictionary learning' to uncover patterns in how combinations of neurons, the mathematical units inside the A.I. model, were activated when Claude was prompted to talk about certain topics."*[82]

But one of the most common causes of AI-related bias is algorithmic curation.

What is the role of algorithmic curation in creating bias?

If you create content or just love scrolling through social media platforms like YouTube, TikTok, or Instagram, then you've likely encountered algorithmic curation. It is essentially the process by which online platforms use AI

---

[81] According to Anthropic's mission statement, its *"...purpose is the responsible development and maintenance of advanced AI for the long-term benefit of humanity."*

[82] Roose, K. (May 21, 2024). AI's Black Boxes Just Got a Little Less Mysterious. The New York Times. Available at *https://www.nytimes.com/2024/05/21/technology/ai-language-models-anthropic.html.*

algorithms to choose, prioritize, and present content for users based on their interests and past behavior. The main actors using algorithmic curation are social media and similar online platforms that have been specifically designed to engage and manipulate users. Many actors and organizations have learned to create content that will raise engagement and therefore has a higher chance of being displayed on newsfeeds. This includes content that feeds anger and rage or is highly biased or polarizing.

This has emerged as a hot topic because these AI algorithms are becoming increasingly sophisticated. Algorithmic curation is determining what we see and don't see on the feeds from social media, online news media, and other platforms.

Algorithmic curation is based on two forms of personalization: explicit and implicit.

- **Explicit personalization** (also called self-selected personalization) is based on the process by which users of an online platform actively opt in and out of information, for example by following other users or selecting into groups.

- **Implicit personalization** occurs when an AI-driven algorithm predicts and responds to user preferences based on past behavior and matches the data with those of other users through collaborative filtering.

Cognitive bias

Being confronted with a different interpretation of the world that challenges your own can cause cognitive stress and bias. Cognitive bias is defined by the Cambridge English

Dictionary as *"the way a particular person understands events, facts, and other people, which is based on their own particular set of beliefs and experiences and may not be reasonable or accurate."*[83]

Cognitive bias is largely unconscious; it's a set of unintentional biases where individuals may be unaware of the resulting attitudes and behaviors. The very fact that most individuals are unaware of their biases is the real source of concern.

---

[83] Cambridge English Dictionary. Available at *https://dictionary.cambridge.org/us/dictionary/english/cognitive-bias.*

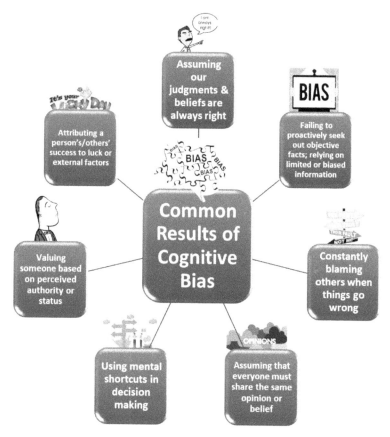

Figure 23: Common Characteristics of Cognitive Bias

Confirmation bias, echo chambers, and filter bubbles

Our brains are great at using past experiences to make quick decisions on the fly, but these shortcuts can also lead to bias. 'Confirmation bias' is our brain's tendency to seek out information that confirms things we already think we know.

In confirmation bias, two things are important to understand: the role that AI algorithmic curation can play in creating and amplifying bias, and whether users are vulnerable to a lack of exposure to diverse content and perspectives.

Social media and other online platforms are incentivized to optimize engagement of users with their platforms by using confirmation bias. As for-profit entities, they earn their incomes by monetizing attention to ads and content they display on the newsfeed. Hence, the content and the user interface are designed to keep users on the platform, including by providing content that is relevant to the user and avoiding content that might drive the user away from the platform such as content that is perceived to challenge users' values or ideology.

An echo chamber occurs when an AI algorithm feeds a person information that reinforces existing biases. Echo chambers are linked more to mechanisms of explicit personalization, created by the election exercised by a user to follow biased accounts or become a member of a group with a clearly biased perspective (creating a biased information menu).

In the case of the filter bubble, the phenomenon is more linked to implicit personalization where users are in a more passive role and are viewed as 'victims' of the AI technology that automatically restricts their exposure to information that might challenge their world view. Filter bubbles and digital echo chambers are therefore seen as one of the main causes of polarization and radicalization online. When users themselves are the main driver in explicit personalization of the data they receive, they may also not possess the ability or even desire to look outside the information they are regularly exposed to. Implicit personalization suggests that the user is not necessarily in charge of the data they receive and is thus more vulnerable to the lack of exposure to diverse content and perspectives.

Many experts are concerned that the AI-powered curation of content on social media platforms limits our chances of encountering and accepting diverse viewpoints. In the words of Sunstein, we might live in *"communication universes in which we hear only what we choose and only what comforts and pleases us."*[84]

What makes individuals vulnerable to bias and misinformation?

Humans have a psychological tendency that makes us more vulnerable to bias. We are 'cognitive misers' which refers to *"the rule that human beings seem to follow [which] is to engage the brain only when all else fails—and usually not even then."*[85]

One source of bias comes from the society in which we live, socialize, and work. When people associate with those they consider peers, the social biases that guide their selection of friends and acquaintances may also strengthen their unconscious or conscious biases.

Another prominent perspective on why humans are prone to be biased or to believe misinformation is referred to as the

---

[84] Sunstein, C., & Sunstein, C. R. *# Republic*. Princeton University Press, 2018.

[85] Why humans are cognitive misers and what it means for the great rationality debate. Rutledge Handbook of Bounded Rationality. Available at *https://ebrary.net/281463/psychology/humans_cognitive_misers_what_great_rationality_debate*.

deficit hypothesis, i.e. individuals may not possess enough knowledge or literacy to distinguish between true and false content.

Additionally, humans generally prefer to avoid exposing themselves to information that challenges their beliefs or that is consistent with their existing worldview.

Humans also fall prey to bias and misinformation, disinformation, and fake news simply because they fail to look for inaccuracy, regardless of their prevailing beliefs.

The effects of AI bias

Before AI, it was humans and organizations that made decisions in recruitment, advertising, law enforcement, criminal sentencing, health care, and banking. Today, many – if not all – of these decisions are made or influenced by AI.

And while AI can promise scale and statistical rigor with unprecedented efficiency, it can also produce bias results. These results can often cause human or societal harm. AI bias can manifest in a number of ways with varying degrees of consequences for those affected.

For most individuals, we look at how humans affect the AI in terms of biased training data and biased AI model output. We don't often consider how these AI biases affect humans. Effects of AI bias are magnified because *"People tend to perceive artificial intelligence algorithms as objective, secure and impartial, but AI algorithms are a product of human design, so they often inherit our mistakes and biases.*"[86]

There are a lot of examples of AI results gone bad. A significant amount of research has indicated that AI bias can damage individuals who are already in marginalized groups. Some impacts may be subtle, such as an AI-driven speech recognition software's inability to understand non-American or minority accents, which might present an inconvenience, especially when using voice-activated digital assistants.

But there are more serious examples. *"Studies have found mortgage algorithms charging Black and Latinx borrowers higher interest rates and egregious cases of recruiting algorithms exacerbating bias against hiring women. A series of studies about various facial recognition software found that most had misidentified darker-skinned women 37% more often than those with lighter-skin tones. A widely used application to predict clinical risk has led to inconsistent referrals by race to specialists, perpetuating racial bias in healthcare. Natural language processing (NLP) models to detect undesirable language online have erroneously censored comments mentioning disabilities, depriving those with disabilities of the opportunity to equally participate in discourse.*"[87]

---

[86] Vincente, L. and Matute, H. (2023). "Humans inherit artificial intelligence biases". Available at *https://www.nature.com/articles/s41598-023-42384-8*.

[87] Best, M. (June 29, 2021). AI bias is personal for me. It should be for you, too. Available at *https://www.pwc.com/us/en/tech-effect/ai-analytics/artificial-intelligence-bias.html*.

Strategies to address AI-based bias

Mitigating bias in AI is essential to preserve trust in our society and between individuals. The McKinsey Global Institute identified six ways AI bias might be addressed. These strategies demonstrate that not all solutions to AI bias must be purely technical in nature.

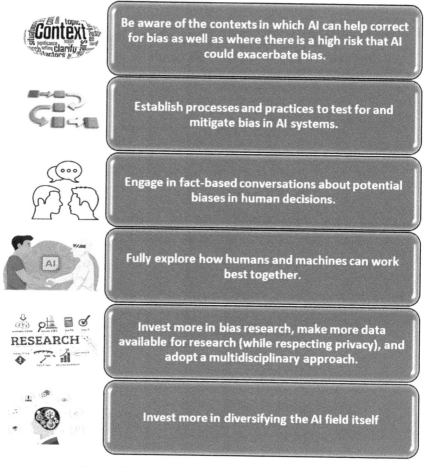

Figure 24: Six Strategies to Address AI Bias[88]

---

[88] Silberg, J. and Manyika, J., (June 6, 2019). Tackling bias in artificial intelligence (and in humans). Available at *https://www.mckinsey.com/featured-insights/artificial-intelligence/tackling-bias-in-artificial-intelligence-and-in-humans.*

1. **Awareness of contexts** where AI has shown a propensity for bias will help developers improve fairness in AI outputs. And AI systems that are developed by more diversified teams are better able to analyze data through various perspectives, making them less likely to repeat historical biases.

2. **Processes and practices to test for AI bias** include establishing and using a portfolio of processes and technical tools and operational practices, such as third-party audits or internal/external 'red teams.' A number of organizations in the AI space are looking at recommendations to aid. These include Google AI (*https://ai.google/responsibility/responsible-ai-practices/*), which provides several best-practice ideas, and IBM's Fairness 360 (*https://github.com/Trusted-AI/AIF360?mhsrc=ibmsearch_a&mhq=fairness%2036 0*), offering a comprehensive set of fairness metrics for data sets and AI models, explanations for these metrics, and algorithms to mitigate bias in both data sets and AI models.

3. **Engage in fact-based conversations** to find bias and address the human-driven attitudes and process that underly it. One form this could take is running algorithms alongside human decision makers, comparing results to help identify what caused the AI model to arrive at a decision to figure out why a certain outcome was achieved.

4. **Look at ways for humans and AI to collaborate**, including 'human-in-the-loop' decision making, where

AI algorithms provide recommendations or options, which humans either select or double-check. This process requires transparency in the AI algorithms.

5. **Conduct more extensive research in AI bias** causes and outputs. Use an interdisciplinary approach involving developers, ethicists, lawmakers, social scientists, and technology experts. Other efforts involve more transparent algorithmic design and embedding ethics in computer science curricula.

6. **Diversify the AI field itself** by engaging communities most likely to be affected by AI bias. This type of work is being done by AI4ALL, a US-based non-profit *"dedicated to increasing diversity and inclusion in AI education, research, development, and policy."*[89]

---

[89] AI4ALL is based on an idea proposed by Dr Olga Russakovsky, a PhD student at Stanford University. See *https://ai-4-all.org/*.

CHAPTER 7: AI AND JOB DISPLACEMENT

> *"Forget artificial intelligence breaking free of human control and taking over the world. A far more pressing concern is how today's generative AI tools will transform the labor market. Some experts envisage a world of increased productivity and job satisfaction; others, a landscape of mass unemployment and social upheaval."*[90]
>
> **Will Knight**

Popular culture often reflects the worry that AI will take over jobs. We see this in dystopian narratives where AI replaces human workers, culminating in societal unrest and economic collapse. These concerns reflect deep-seated fears about advances in AI and the potential impact on the workforce. The anxiety about job loss was only exacerbated by the emergence of generative AI, which has shown strong abilities in areas formerly reserved for human workers.

In contrast to these dire predictions, a recent study completed by the Massachusetts Institute of Technology (MIT) suggests *"... that AI job displacement will be substantial, but also*

---

[90] Knight, W. (April 11, 2024). "No One Actually Knows How AI Will Affect Jobs". Available at *https://www.wired.com/story/ai-impact-on-work-mary-daly-interview/.*

gradual – and therefore there is room for policy and retraining to mitigate unemployment impacts. ["]91

% of Jobs at Potential Loss to AI

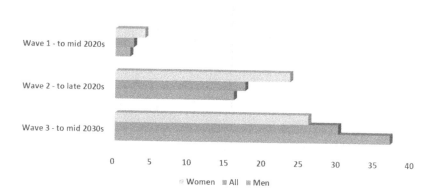

Figure 25: % of Jobs at Potential Loss to AI[92]

Contrast the MIT study with the results of research conducted by Goldman Sacks, which postulated that *"a new wave of AI systems may also have a major impact on employment markets around the world. Shifts in workflows*

---

91 Svanberg, M., et al. (January 18, 2024). Beyond AI Exposure: Which Tasks are Cost-Effective to Automate with Computer Vision. Available at *https://futuretech-site.s3.us-east-2.amazonaws.com/2024-01-18+Beyond_AI_Exposure.pdf*.

92 Adapted from Accenture Report. (2024). Technology Vision 2024. Available at *https://www.accenture.com/content/dam/accenture/final/accenture-com/document-2/Accenture-Tech-Vision-2024.pdf#zoom=40*.

triggered by these advances could expose the equivalent of 300 million full-time jobs to automation."[93]

The International Monetary Fund (IMF) in a staff discussion note of January 2024 stated: *"Almost 40 percent of global employment is exposed to AI, with advanced economies at greater risk but also better poised to exploit AI benefits than emerging market and developing economies. In advanced economies, about 60 percent of jobs are exposed to AI, due to prevalence of cognitive-task-oriented jobs."*[94]

These somewhat contrasting viewpoints highlight the challenges of predicting the impact of AI and generative AI on jobs. Nevertheless, it is a certainty that AI will have some level of impact on job security in 2024 and beyond.

One of the areas that may be most affected by the recent developments in AI is the cognitive class.

Job displacement and the cognitive class

The cognitive class is defined as professionals whose work primarily involves thinking and problem-solving, such as analysts, managers, and knowledge workers, and which has long been considered immune to the disruptive forces of technology. AI, however, is changing this formula. While

---

[93] Goldman Sachs. (April 5, 2023). "Generative AI could raise global GDP by 7%". Available at *https://www.goldmansachs.com/intelligence/pages/generative-ai-could-raise-global-gdp-by-7-percent.html.*

[94] Cazzinaga, M., et al. (January 2024). Gen-AI: Artificial Intelligence and the Future of Work. Available at *https://www.imf.org/en/Publications/Staff-Discussion-Notes/Issues/2024/01/14/Gen-AI-Artificial-Intelligence-and-the-Future-of-Work-542379?cid=bl-com-SDNEA2024001.*

cognitive thinkers and professionals have enjoyed relative job security throughout multiple technological advances due to the complex nature of their work, the capabilities of generative AI is encroaching upon their domain, forcing them to re-evaluate their skills, and approach to their careers.

For several centuries, changes in prevailing technologies have changed the face of the workplace. Yet in the past, technological developments most often appeared to affect the 'blue collar' or working class. For example, robots in assembly-line vehicle production became increasingly commonplace in the latter part of the twentieth century. Automated robots were used to perform simple, repetitive tasks, thereby helping to increase output and standardize production quality while reducing cost. Assembly line jobs passed from humans to robots, but retraining created new, more complex jobs for humans to fill.

Clearly, the increased development and deployment of AI will not be the first time the world has experienced significant shifts in employment due to new technology. History tells us that in the long run, technology is a net creator of jobs. But our societal psychology is conditioned to think of lower-skilled workers as the first victims of the AI technologies. To keep alive this preconception, we are not somewhat misguided about the class of workers who are at the highest risk of marginalization or job loss.

The difference in the age of AI and especially generative AI is that many of the jobs most likely to be threatened by AI are those of the 'cognitive class' – those whose jobs are based on knowledge, research, analysis, and/or writing skills. *"Surprisingly enough, knowledge workers are facing the highest level of exposure here, which is quite different with what we've seen with other revolutions. With automation, often it was manual labor that was replaced. Unlike previous cycles of technical innovation, in-person, often low-wage jobs that rely heavily on humans being physically present are likely to be the most resilient to encroaching AI. "*[95]

Figure 26: AI Job Displacement and The Cognitive Class[96]

Researchers at OpenAI, which developed ChatGPT, analyzed 19,256 tasks performed by 923 workers at various educational and skill levels in the US. The research indicated that sophisticated AI models could perform at least some of

[95] Cerullo, M. (January 24, 2024). How the AI revolution is different: It threatens white collar workers. CBS MoneyWatch. Available at *https://www.cbsnews.com/news/what-is-generative-ai-job-exposure/,*
[96] Jeff Parker. Available at *https://politicalcartoons.com/.*

the tasks executed by 80% of American workers. And Sam Altman, OpenAI's CEO, said that *"Jobs are definitely going to go away, full stop."*[97]

The same research indicated that only 4% of jobs had no tasks that could be augmented or replaced by AI technology. These job categories included construction workers, gardeners, athletes, specific types of care work, and others in some of the lower-skilled groups as well as certain jobs requiring human creativity and problem solving.

Why is the cognitive class at risk?

Historically, new technological developments predominantly affected routine, lower-skilled tasks. But as a result of AI's capabilities to encompass higher-level cognitive functions, such as code writing, occupations previously considered exempt from displacement or modification by AI due to their complexity and dependence on deep expertise now face potential disruption.

It's not all doom and gloom, however. AI will not be creating significant job displacement in the near future, leaving us time to develop and implement strategies for mitigating the potential of job loss.

AI and inequality

Alexandre Fasel stated: *"AI is amongst the key technologies of our time and will have a lasting impact on society,*

---

[97] Anderson, R. (July 24, 2023). Does Sam Altman Know What He's Creating? The Atlantic. Available at *https://www.theatlantic.com/magazine/archive/2023/09/sam-altman-openai-chatgpt-gpt-4/674764/.*

economies and politics and an important role to play in tackling the global challenges we face. Not all countries have the same access to the resources needed to implement these. If we do not address this, AI could become a driver of inequality."[98]

There is potential for a period of job displacement as AI becomes more and more adept at certain job-related skills. *"Technological advances since World War II have generated 'skill-biased technological change,' which is when technological innovation increases demand for more-educated workers, leading to labor-market polarization. In the postwar era, workers who knew how to operate sophisticated machinery (and later, computers, the internet, and related technologies) found themselves in high demand, while those who lacked those skills had a harder time finding employment. Many traditional tasks could be automated or executed more efficiently using first machines and then computer technology.*"[99]

Like the post-Second World War technologies, an increase in AI-based technologies will also inevitably change labor markets, and those changes may introduce increased inequality – within and across nations.

And inequality is a destructive force.

---

[98] Alexandre Fasel is the state secretary and Switzerland's special representative for science diplomacy. This statement was made at the World Economic Forum Annual Meeting at Davos in 2024.
[99] Bell, S. and Korinek, A. (October 2023). "AI's Economic Peril". Journal of Democracy, Vol. 34, Issue 4. Available at *https://www.dropbox.com/scl/fi/nkug14sy12hrdacgu8ujk/JoD_manuscript.pdf?rlkey=b5s1b4bowav11ikl9kcant79h&e=1&dl=0.*

Inequality and democratic institutions

Democratic institutions and governments are more frequently called into question when inequality increases. The existence – or even perception – of high inequality breeds discontent and propagates division among citizens – notably between the 'ordinary' people and the political or economic elites.

It is not uncommon for governments to provide public services in an unequal manner, for instance by offering excellent services to the richer neighborhoods while failing those that are poorer.

The digital divide

Many workers and even nations do not have access to the technologies that will allow them to be part of the new economy. The term for this lack of access is 'digital divide.'

Demographic and socioeconomic factors play a key role in the digital divide and, more specifically, the AI divide. Studies suggest that the most disadvantaged and vulnerable users in today's digital age are the elderly, the less educated, women, demographics with lower income, and ethnic minorities.

In recent years, digital competence, which includes the knowledge, skills, attitudes, abilities, strategies, and awareness required when using digital technologies, has gained significance. With the rise of AI technologies, AI-related competence has emerged as a frontier within digital competence. Considering the increasing societal influence of AI, many researchers and scholars are exploring the intersection of the digital divide and AI.

Like every previous disruptive change – the invention of the Internet, access to broadband, and the mobile revolution fueled by smart devices – the opportunities enabled by AI leaves those without Internet access and within the digital divide ever further behind just by staying in place. Urgent action is needed to bridge the digital divide and promote equitable access to AI technologies, or billions of people across the globe will be unable to benefit from this technology while still suffering its disruptions.

So, what's the role of AI in inequality?

AI is already affecting job availability, salaries, and job quality – all of which will have consequences for broader economic inequality. AI-based systems can automate and substitute for workers in numerous types of jobs, resulting in decreased labor demand and depressed wages. Most empirical studies find that AI-based technologies will not decrease overall employment in the long term. These technologies, however, are very likely to lessen the comparative income going to lower-skilled labor, which will expand inequality across society.

Generative AI and inequality

While no one can accurately predict the results of the expansion of generative AI, it's possible that it might even reduce the contemporary societal problem of income inequality based on an analysis by MIT Sloan School Associate Professor Nathan Wilmers.[100]

---

[100] Wilmers, N. (March 27, 2024). Generative AI and the Future of Inequality. Available at *https://mit-genai.pubpub.org/pub/24gsgdjx/release/1?readingCollection=bc5ea8fc*

Generative AI is fairly new, and direct research into the mid- and long-term effects is in the early stages. But there are indications that GenAI technologies may affect the workforce and social inequality in a much different way than other Internet and AI-based technologies. *"The construction of internet infrastructure offers a well-studied example of technological effects on inequality. Broadband internet roll-out improves labor market outcomes for high-skilled workers, while worsening outcomes for lower skill workers (Akerman, et al. 2015). It exacerbates inequality between rich and poor localities (Forman, et al. 2012). Likewise, firms implementing new information technologies increase demand for skilled labor (Bresnahan, et al. 2002), and technologies like these facilitated the rise of superstar firms (Autor, et al. 2020). Different research designs, addressing different facets of information technology and considering related but distinct outcomes, all suggest that these technologies have tended to increase inequality by concentrating benefits on already advantaged workers, firms, and cities"*[101]

Early indications are that generative AI technologies will have a large effect on the cognitive class, as we discussed in an earlier chapter. *"It is white-collar positions, rather than blue-collar, service, and other frontline jobs, that are composed of tasks most immediately exposed to disruption by generative AI. If this disruption involves more task substitution than augmentation, then at the level of broad occupation categories, generative AI tools could reduce*

---

[101] Wilmers, 2024.

demand in white-collar jobs relative to blue-collar and in-person service jobs."[102]

What does this mean? Increased use of generative AI could have a leveling effect on income and societal inequality by reducing the pay gaps between 'skilled' and 'unskilled' workers. This evolution could challenge the current economic dominance of university-educated, higher-paid white-collar workers.

Some may see this as a rosy scenario, but there is reason for pessimism. Wilmers identified several potential negative outcomes for the increased implementation of generative AI:

1. A decline in the demand for cognitive workers could create an influx of white-collar workers competing for a decreased supply of jobs. Without retraining and the creation of new job categories to absorb these workers, there could be technological unemployment that could reverberate across multiple sectors.

2. Generative AI may reshape the distribution of high- and lower-paying businesses. Generative AI has the potential to contribute to corporate growth of 'technology giants' through innovation, perhaps reducing the ability of smaller businesses to succeed.

3. The use of AI to monitor employees is already showing its effects in a post-COVID-19 world. The sense of being monitored and surveilled affects trust between the employer and the employee, as well as the potential for negative psychological effects. Generative AI may

---

[102] Wilmers, 2024.

facilitate the monitoring of individual employee activity and performance. Increased surveillance could further enhance feelings of inequality in the workforce and in society.

Strategies to reduce the effects of AI-generated job displacement

Understanding which job categories are the most vulnerable to job loss due to AI is crucial in designing strategies that can mitigate those effects. For those professionals in the cognitive class, it's essential to participate in continual learning and upskilling.

To prepare all workers for the potential changes due to AI, there are a number of suggested avenues:

1. **Create educational and retraining opportunities**: Integrate AI concepts into curricula at multiple grade levels, fostering creativity and problem-solving skills, and emphasizing the importance of ethics and responsible AI use. At the same time, provide opportunities for learning and retraining outside the classroom for adult workers whose jobs have been displaced by AI.

2. **Work to eliminate the digital divide**: Mitigate or eliminate the digital divide within and across nations by providing equitable access to digital technologies.

3. **Pass appropriate legislation and regulations**: Encourage governments and other agencies to establish legal and policy frameworks for responsible AI development and deployment.

4. **Evolve along with AI**: Seize the opportunity to develop complementary skill sets that allow workers to collaborate and grow along with AI technologies.

5. **Anticipate the potential impacts**: Prepare for the impacts to workers and look to opportunities to prevent social and political instability as a result of job displacement.

CHAPTER 8: AI IMITATION IS NOT A FORM OF FLATTERY

> *"Copyright law is created to incentivize human creativity. Clearly, right now, AI is not doing that. It's hurting human creativity."*[103]
>
> **Shawn Shan**

The protection of intellectual property (IP) has social and individual benefits. On the one hand, it protects the rights of creators to the content they create and it incentivizes the further production of innovative, valuable, intangible, and – in the digital world and AI – easily copied works. The statement was made that digital and AI-based replication is not creation. Luke Savage said: *"Artificial intelligence is poised to suck the soul out of art – and make artists' already precarious existence even worse."*[104]

Let's talk about intellectual property and copyright law

Intellectual property (IP) is any unique content created using human intellect often with a monetary value. IP can be books, music, art, inventions, chemical formulae, or

---

[103] Shawn Sahn is the Glaze project lead, University of Chicago, Department of Computer Science.
[104] Savage, L. (May 31, 2023). "Reproduction Isn't Creativity, and AI Isn't Art". Jacobin online. Available at *https://jacobin.com/2023/05/ai-artificial-intelligence-art-creativity-reproduction-capitalism*.

information system code. In most parts of the world, there is a common understanding that individuals have a right to own property – including the results of their own labor. The two most important reasons for protection of IP are legal and ethical:

Figure 27: Why IP is Protected

Legal reasons for IP and copyright protection

There are a number of ways IP is protected under law – at least in the US:

- **Trade secrets** – IP that can provide a company with a competitive advantage. Examples include processes, proprietary designs, customer lists, and certain collections of information.

- **Trademarks and service marks** – these are usually a word, symbol, or picture used by an organization to identify a service or an item. By obtaining a trademark, a company has the right to use that symbol and prevent other companies from using it. For example, the brand name of Coca-Cola has a trademark and associated protections.

- **Patents** – exclusive rights to IP given by the US government to an inventor. This differs from a trademark in that a patent is a public document providing a detailed description of the invention.

- **Copyright** – provided to content developers, such as authors, which gives certain rights to the original works. The owner of the copyright has the sole right to reproduce the copyrighted work, distribute copies, display copies in public, perform the work in public, and develop new works based on the copyrighted work.

Internationally, there are similarities and differences in laws governing the protection of IP and copyright. Protection against unauthorized use in a particular country is governed by the national laws of that country; in other words, copyright protection is subject to the laws in that specific country where protection is sought. Under UK law, for example, copyright protection is governed by the Copyright, Designs and Patents Act 1988 (the 1988 Act), as amended.

Copyright and IP protection in the EU is based on a complex set of laws and agreements. Many of the EU directives on IP and copyright protection are in accordance with various member obligations under the Berne Convention and the Rome Convention, as well as the obligations of the EU and its Member States under the World Trade Organization 'TRIPS' Agreement and the two 1996 World Intellectual

Property Organisation (WIPO) Internet Treaties (the WIPO Copyright Treaty and the WIPO Performances and Phonograms Treaty). While we won't address these in any detail here, it is clear that IP and copyright protection is recognized by the EU member states. More information on these treaties and agreements can be found at *https://www.copyright.gov/international-issues/*.

Ethical reasons for IP and copyright protection

Think about this: You created 'intellectual property', for example a song, and it wound up online. Wouldn't you want others to give you credit for your original work? Let's say they reproduced it and made money off it – and no one knew you were the original creator. That could create an ethical dilemma.

IP and copyright protection also benefits society as a whole. It promotes the spread of knowledge and culture by ensuring that creators are recognized, and perhaps even remunerated, for their contributions.

Why is the protection of IP and copyright important?

Protection of IP and copyright protection plays an important role in incentivizing and stimulating the creation of many intellectual works. Without this protection, it would be simple for others to exploit the works of others without paying any royalties or remuneration to the creator of the work.

The authors of the US Constitution recognized the positive benefits of protection of IP and encouraging creativity. Article I, Section 8 gives Congress the power to *"promote the Progress of Science and useful Arts by security for limited Times to Authors and Inventors the exclusive Right to their respective Writings and Discoveries.* " Over the years since the original crafting of the constitution, there has been copyright 'creep,' extending the types of protected IP that are protected by copyright and the length of the copyright protection period to advance with the times.

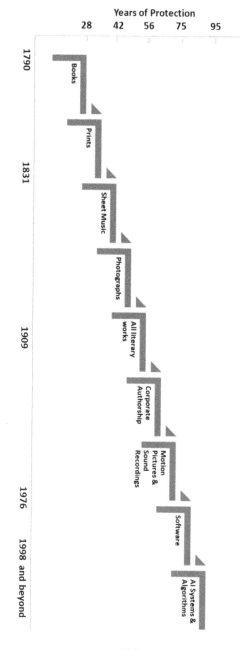

Figure 28: Copyright Creep

Protection of IP and copyright continues to play an important role in the digital age. At the same time, ensuring these protections are respected has become increasingly more challenging, especially with the advent of generative AI.

The results of IP protection and copyright are not always positive. Many contend that these protections are outdated in our digital world and that there are more negatives than positives.

Pros and cons of IP and copyright protection

IP and copyright protection continue to play a critical role in a digital world. But IP and copyright protections, while they are an essential tool, also have their drawbacks – especially today.

Pros and Cons of IP and Copyright Protection

Pros	Cons
• Creators can control reproduction, distribution, and display of their work, and profit from their creations • Incentivizes creators to innovate and fosters competition • Ensures creators receive fair compensation for their work • Creators are credited for their work and others are deterred from appropriating or copying their ideas without permission or acknowledgment • Grants creators moral rights to their work	• Excessive protection can suppress innovation, while weak protection discourages creativity • Global copyright coordination is an ongoing challenge to ensure that IP is protected consistently • Use limitations can restrict the ability of others to build on existing works or ideas, resulting in a stifling of new innovation • Limited access and licensing costs under copyright laws can restrict the availability of valuable resources to others

Figure 29: Pros and Cons of IP and Copyright Protection

How has the digital age and AI impacted IP and copyright protection?

Let's say I have a university paper due. It's common today for me to scroll through the Internet to find other papers, images, videos, etc. And since I found it and it's easy to copy, I might think it's mine to use. But that's not the case.

The digital world has transformed the way content is created, consumed, and distributed. The rise of digital technologies, such as social media, smart devices, and the Internet, has made it easier than ever to use and share digital content. This has given rise to a number of challenges to IP and copyright.

The ease of copying and distributing digital content has made it extremely difficult to prevent piracy and IP/copyright infringement. And, because of the way information traverses our digital platforms, assigning ownership and enforcing copyright laws can be a complex and costly process.

AI and its impact on the protection of IP and copyright

Although there were already challenges to the protection of IP, the emergence of AI and generative AI in particular has created a very new set of issues. Advances in AI are raising questions about how copyright law principles such as authorship, infringement, and fair use will apply to content created or used by AI.

The first question becomes – does AI training infringe on IP protections and copyright? It seems that some problems are generated by the way AI and generative AI are trained. Generative AI systems are 'trained' to create literary, visual, and other artistic works by ingesting large amounts of data, which may include text, images, and other works downloaded from the Internet – usually without permission from the creators. This training process may also involve making digital copies of existing works. The training material includes large, publicly available content that often includes copyrighted works. The process requires making copies of the data to be analyzed, and creating these copies without specific permission from the creator may infringe on the exclusive right to make reproductions of their work.

The second and equally important question is – do the outputs from AI constitute infringement on copyrights? AI and generative AI are often critiqued for infringing on copyrights by generating content that reuses, mimics, or resembles existing works.

Ever since AI and generative AI emerged and allowed users to create images, music, and textual content based on prompts and queries, the use of these AI tools has become increasingly popular. Some of the content created mimics that of existing artists. *"This has caused a lot of harm to artists, as documented by the University of Chicago Department of Computer Science's Glaze project in a study of 1,000 artists. The research finds that AI mimicking artists in this way sabotages the artists' business model by displacing the original art in search results and demoralizes art students who see future career paths eliminated."*[105]

As a result of the rapid emergence of generative AI, many claim that piracy has fully entered the age of AI. With both text-based and image-based generative AI tools trained on copyrighted work and often creating output that is very similar to it, several different lawsuits have been filed that

---

[105] Info-Tech Research Group. "Tech Trends 2024". Deloitte. Available at *https://www2.deloitte.com/us/en/insights/focus/tech-trends.html.*

could have major impacts on the field of generative AI. Here are just a few examples:

- A class-action lawsuit against GitHub, Microsoft, and OpenAI targets the GitHub Copilot tool. Coders say that Copilot is copying and republishing code without attribution. That's against the GitHub open-source license. Microsoft and GitHub have tried to have this case dismissed but were unsuccessful, and will face the allegations in court.

- A lawsuit against Stability AI, Midjourney, and DeviantArt alleges these companies scraped the web and infringed on artists' copyrights by training their AI models.

- Getty Images filed a copyright complaint against Stability AI for allegedly copying and processing millions of its images and metadata.

- Authors Paul Tremblay and Mona Awad are suing OpenAI for allegedly infringing on authors' copyrights. The suit estimates more than 300,000 books were copied in OpenAI's training data.

- Sarah Silverman is suing Meta and OpenAI, claiming that their large language models illegally acquired data sets that included her work.[106]

And this is just the tip of the iceberg.

---

[106] Info-Tech Research Group. "Tech Trends 2024". Deloitte. Available at *https://www2.deloitte.com/us/en/insights/focus/tech-trends.html*.

Based on these and many other lawsuits, the courts have decried that content from AI and generative AI cannot be considered copyrighted works, but they can make imitative works of existing artists' content, and this new content has the potential for infringing on another artist's copyrights.

Fair use and transformative use

Creators of original works have questioned whether the companies creating the AI models have a legal right to use their works. The US and Europe have different approaches to copyright and intellectual property.

US copyright law is based on a utilitarian rationale for copyright protection concerned with amplifying welfare of the public. It is intended to serve the maximum dissemination of works while incentivizing creation. Europe gives more value to the creative process and is intended to provide individuals control over their intellectual property.

In the US, the answer is based on a determination of fair use and a concept within it called transformative use. The Fair Use Doctrine permits the exploitation of an intellectual property or a copyrighted work *"for purposes such as criticism, comment, news reporting, teaching (including multiple copies for classroom use), scholarship, or research."*[107]

The Fair Use Doctrine includes something called 'transformative use.' Broadly interpreted, this means that copyrighted content can be used to create something new and

---

[107] 17 U.S. Code § 107 - Limitations on exclusive rights: Fair use. Available at *https://www.law.cornell.edu/uscode/text/17/107*.

novel, such as training an AI to create new artworks. Google used the fair use argument in response to a lawsuit about scanning books into an AI and displaying pieces of the original content in the results of the AI model. Google won the lawsuit using transformative use as the basis of its argument. This has undoubtably set a precedent that many generative AI companies will rely on when they inevitably end up in court for IP and copyright violations.

But let's toss in a new thought: "Everything is a Remix," as suggested by Kirby Ferguson in his YouTube video.[108] This is an update to the famous quote by Mark Twain: *"There is no such thing as a new idea. It is impossible. We simply take a lot of old ideas and put them into a sort of mental kaleidoscope. We give them a turn and they make new and curious combinations. We keep on turning and making new combinations indefinitely; but they are the same old pieces of colored glass that have been in use through all the ages."*[109]

Here is an example of AI-generated art that clearly harks back to van Gogh's famous Starry Night:

---

[108] See the Kirby Ferguson YouTube video at
https://www.youtube.com/watch?v=nJPERZDfyWc.
[109] Twain, M. *Mark Twain's Own Autobiography: The Chapters from the North American Review.* Available on Amazon at
https://www.amazon.com/Mark-Twains-Own-Autobiography-Wisconsin/dp/0299234746.

8: AI imitation is not a form of flattery

Figure 30: AI-generated Art[110]

At first glance, the similarity is clear. But on closer examination, you can easily see that this might be claimed as 'transformative.'

Kirby Ferguson traces the concept of remix back to music, specifically hip hop. But essentially the term 'remix' as defined by Wikipedia means *"piece of media which has been altered or contorted from its original state by adding, removing, or changing pieces of the item."* And this resembles how AI/generative AI arrives at a new piece of content output. It takes training data, reinterprets, changes, incorporates, and provides new content in the form of art,

---

[110] A Vincent van Gogh-inspired Google Deep Dream painting. Artnet. Available at *https://news.artnet.com/market/google-inceptionism-art-sells-big-439352*.

music, or literature. So, what is the problem? Is this not a form of legitimate remix?

The problem lies in attribution. Human users employ these AI, and most recently generative AI systems, for various purposes, including academic or non-academic research, preparing assignments, and understanding complex problems. For example, lawyers may use AI to scan reams of legal documents to research legal questions and draft briefs, thus reducing the lawyer's workload. Generative AI models are trained on materials that even contain parts of IP or copyrighted works that are included in the training data. But generative AI does not provide attribution for the copyrighted works that may be used to create a certain output.

And if a generative AI is asked to provide attribution, it may not be correct or even real. This was the situation with New York lawyer Steven A. Schwartz, who submitted an AI-generated brief to the Federal District Court in New York. The other party's lawyers were unable to find the legal documents cited in Schwartz's brief. When requested to provide additional information about the cited cases, Schwartz went back to the generative AI and submitted the generated output to the court, where it was revealed that the cited cases did not even exist. They were made up by the AI system.[111]

---

[111] Weiser, B. and Schweber, N. (June 8, 2023). "The ChatGPT Lawyer Explains Himself". The New York Times. Available at *https://www.nytimes.com/2023/06/08/nyregion/lawyer-chatgpt-sanctions.html.*

8: AI imitation is not a form of flattery

AI and education

"In colleges and universities, we've been sort of obsessed with A.I. technology because for a lot of people, it poses little challenges like plagiarism and it sort of devalues the ability to do original work. So, it's something that gets talked about a lot on universities,"[112] according to Tom St. Antoine in an interview with Fox News.

In just over a year, ChatGPT and generative AI have progressed from a basic awareness to a center of attention for many higher-education institutions across the nation and worldwide. Within weeks after its release at the end of 2022, there was extensive use by students at all grade levels. This inevitably raised serious questions about academic integrity and about the potential effects on student learning. Concern around the ability of generative AI to create quality assignment responses grew with the release of GPT-4 in 2023, which demonstrates almost human-level performance on multiple professional and academic benchmarks – and sometimes even better.

Because of generative AI's ability to imitate human abilities to produce outputs in text, images, videos, music, and software code, millions of individuals are now using it in education and knowledge production, which has potentially huge repercussions for education, as it replaces the higher-order research and analysis that constitutes the basis of human learning.

---

[112] Dr Tom St. Antoine is the Palm Beach Atlantic University professor of communication and Supper Honors Program director. His comments are available at *https://www.foxnews.com/media/will-ai-end-education-economist-predicts-schools-teachers-could-become-obsolete.*

The initial concern of many educators, including myself, was that students would 'cheat' on their assignments. The second, and more overwhelming, concern is that students would undermine their own ability to think and learn. We also realized that its use by students was inevitable, and that we had to adapt our teaching philosophy to embrace and encourage the ethical use of generative AI tools.

In spite of the potential for positive application of generative AI in education, several concerns for students remain:

- **Hallucinations** – false answers are sometimes generated as a result of models using 'statistics' to pick the next word with no 'understanding' of content.
- **Subpar training data** – data could be insufficient, obsolete, or contain sensitive information and biases, leading to biased, prohibited, or incorrect responses.
- **Copyright violations** – some models have been accused of using copyrighted data for training purposes, which is then reused without appropriate permission.
- **Deepfakes** – outputs generated by ChatGPT could appear realistic but may be fake content.
- **Fraud and abuse** – bad actors are exploiting ChatGPT by writing fake reviews, spamming, and phishing.[113]

---

[113] Sheehan, T. (September 11, 2023). "Generative AI in Education: Past, Present, and Future". Available at *https://er.educause.edu/articles/sponsored/2023/9/generative-ai-in-education-past-present-and-future.*

Strategies to avoid inappropriate AI imitation

To reduce violations of copyright, intellectual property, and plagiarism as a result of AI and generative AI, there are a number of suggested strategies:

1. **Control and restrict inappropriate student and staff use** and train faculty members to encourage appropriate student exploration and evaluation.
2. **Use anti-plagiarism tools** that are designed to detect content copied or created by AI and generative AI.
3. **Speed up the creation of lesson plans**, teaching videos, images, presentations, lecture notes, and study support materials that address the use of AI and generative AI at work and in the classroom.
4. **Develop and continually refine policies** to promote internal exploration of how to leverage AI and generative AI in a way that respects intellectual property and copyright.
5. **Develop tools** to quickly detect and report on content that is clearly AI generated.
6. **Foster an environment of creativity and innovation** that balances restrictions to protect creators and permissions that reward creators, while also enabling others to make new things – even if these things are AI generated.
7. **Create research groups** to explore technical solutions to the attribution problem in AI and generative AI.
8. **Use tools to help AI models** comply with copyright laws and ensure creators are properly compensated.

CHAPTER 9: DIGITAL TECHNOLOGY, AI, AND PRIVACY – IS ANYTHING REALLY PRIVATE ANYMORE?

> *"As artificial intelligence evolves, it magnifies the ability to use personal information in ways that can intrude on privacy interests by raising analysis of personal information to new levels of power and speed."*[114]
>
> **Cameron F. Kerry**

In 1928, Supreme Court Justice Louis Brandeis defined privacy as "the right to be left alone":

The makers of our Constitution undertook to secure conditions favorable to the pursuit of happiness. ... They knew that only a part of the pain, pleasure and satisfaction of life are to be found in material things. ... They sought to protect Americans in their beliefs, their thoughts, their emotions and their sensations. They conferred, as against the government, the right to be left alone—the most

---

[114] Kerry, C. (February 10, 2020). Protecting privacy in an AI-driven world. Brookings Institution. Available at *https://www.brookings.edu/articles/protecting-privacy-in-an-ai-driven-world/*.

comprehensive of rights and the right most valued by civilized men.[115]

Academics and researchers have identified privacy as one of the conditions essential for the development of individual identity, for the establishment of intimacy, and even for the functioning of democratic institutions.

So, what is the definition of privacy? Beyond the simple definition from Brandeis of the right to be left alone, there are several forms of privacy, including the following:

1. **Privacy of person** – bodily privacy; privacy for physical/medical choice
2. **Privacy of personal behavior** – privacy of religion, politics, social media activity, etc.
3. **Privacy of personal communications** – privacy for mail or digital communications; freedom from interception
4. **Privacy of personal data** – data information privacy, control of use/dissemination of personal data

AI and its effect on privacy

Personal privacy can be a difficult concept to define as it is both multidimensional – affecting one or more of the above forms of privacy – and very situational. One taxonomy of

---

[115] Dissent in Olmstead v. U.S. (1928). Since then, the Supreme Court has delineated a constitutionally protected *"right to privacy,"* which includes both an *"individual interest in avoiding* disclosure of personal matters" and an *"interest in independence in making certain kinds of important decisions."* Whalen v. Roe (1977).

information privacy harms includes physical, economic, reputational, emotional, and relational harms to individuals.[116]

These privacy harms are related to our ability to understand and manage the digital technologies and AI systems and prevent damage to individual autonomy. This is related to a real or perceived inability to make informed choices, the inability to correct data, and a general lack of control over how personal information is gathered and used. Let's consider privacy policies on the average social media or online platform.

Here are a few of the issues with privacy policies that are only exacerbated through the integration of AI:

- The policies are often written in 'legalese' and filled with technical and legal jargon
- The privacy policy is not up front on the online platform and not easily accessible from every page
- The policy is not updated to keep pace with current technologies in use on the platform
- The online platform assumes consent and does not provide for an explicit opt in or opt out
- Too many still use a 2000s-era format: big words, tiny print, and enormous and almost illegible blocks of text

"So, each and every Internet user, were they to read every privacy policy on every website they visit would spend 25

---

[116] Keats Citron, D. and Solove, D. J. (2022). "Privacy Harms". Boston University Law Review 102. Available at *https://scholarship.law.gwu.edu/faculty_publications/1534/*.

days out of the year just reading privacy policies! If it was your job to read privacy policies for 8 hours per day, it would take you 76 work days to complete the task. Nationalized, that's 53.8 BILLION HOURS of time required to read privacy policies."[117]

Combined with the rapid advances in AI technology, the way we interact with the world is also changing. Ranging from our use of personal and home smart technology, to targeted advertising on social media, to chatbots that respond to our customer service inquiries, AI is increasingly integrated into our daily lives. Even though these developments can certainly be convenient, they also raise serious concerns about privacy.

The reason for increased privacy concerns is AI technology is designed to collect, analyze, and store massive amounts of data – including personal data, which can be used in ways that compromise individual privacy. This data is often collected and stored, transferred, or used by AI systems without an individual's explicit knowledge or consent, which raises serious questions about transparency and control over personal information.

Data forms the baseline for all AI systems. Future digital technology and AI development will continue to increase the need for increased amounts of training data, feeding an even greater competition for data acquisition than we have seen in

---

[117] Madrigal, A. (March 1, 2012). Reading the Privacy Policies You Encounter in a Year Would Take 76 Work Days. The Atlantic. Available at
https://www.theatlantic.com/technology/archive/2012/03/reading-the-privacy-policies-you-encounter-in-a-year-would-take-76-work-days/253851/.

the past few years. This largely unconstrained data collection poses significant risks to privacy that extend beyond the individual level – in the aggregate, it poses societal-level harms that cannot be addressed sufficiently through the application of individual data rights alone.

And because of digital and AI technologies, businesses, government, law enforcement, online platforms, and many more now know more about our personal lives than we ever thought possible: who we are, what we like, where we go, what we do, with whom we do these things, and often even what we think and feel.

Privacy concerns are not limited to individuals. Digital and AI systems can be the source for larger-scale societal risks precisely because they collect and analyze data at scale, taking in tremendous amounts of data and in turn creating connections and outcomes previously impossible through other processes. Through this enhanced capability, digital and AI technologies have the potential for classifying and applying decisional outcomes to large groups of the population based on gender, demographic, or other affiliation – and thus intensifying social biases for specific groups.

"The expectation that your data will be gathered at every turn, the powerlessness of being unable to do anything about it, and the lack of transparency about how one's data is used or decisions are made about you all feed a growing sense of inevitability that data privacy has already been lost."[118] This

---

[118] Draper, N. and Turow, J. (March 8, 2019). "The corporate cultivation of digital resignation". New Media & Society 21(8). Available at *https://journals.sagepub.com/doi/full/10.1177/1461444819833331.*

sense of inevitability is heightened by the proliferation of digital and AI applications that are collecting our data.

Common digital and AI applications and privacy concerns

There are a number of specific AI applications that raise unique privacy concerns. Virtual assistants, such as Alexa and Siri, and smart speakers can record and store audio data from individuals' homes or their personal smart devices. Sure, these devices offer convenience, but the potential for unintended data collection and misuse of personal information is a growing concern.

Facial recognition technology (FRT) is another AI technology that raises privacy concerns, particularly in the context of law enforcement and surveillance. The use of this technology, especially in public places, can result in the collection of biometric data without an individual's express knowledge or consent, and raises significant questions about the ability to maintain anonymity and privacy.

Social media and targeted advertising also pose significant privacy risks, since they collect and monetize personal data to create targeted advertisements that can be highly personalized and often difficult to opt out of – even when offered the option.

The increase in autonomous vehicles (AVs) and the development of smart cities also has raised concerns about the collection and use of location and sensor data and the possibility that this information could be misused or hacked.

Generative AI and privacy

It would not be an overstatement to say that the emergence of generative AI has substantially shifted the terms of the privacy debate. Wonder at the capabilities of image generators, such as Midjourney and DALL-E, or large language models (LLMs), such as ChatGPT and Copilot, has also raised questions about how generative AI capabilities are being developed and what data is being used to support them. As it became more widely understood that generative systems predominantly rely on data scraped from across the Internet, concerns escalated about exactly what data – and whose data – was behind these systems.

The very fact that many generative systems are largely built on scraped data has raised questions about whether and under what contexts data-scraping practices can be compliant with existing privacy laws, such as the GDPR, particularly when personally identifiable information may be embedded in training data, even if that data is publicly available.

Nations are taking action. For example, on March 20, 2023, the Italian data protection authority (the Garante) received a report that OpenAI – the company that developed GPT-4, the AI model that is the basis for ChatGPT – experienced a breach of user data. The Garante swiftly launched an investigation, which found that OpenAI was collecting user-generated data to train its AI model, including users' conversations and information on payments by subscribers to the service. It deemed the collection of this data to train ChatGPT's language model unlawful under the GDPR. On March 31, 2023, the Garante demanded that OpenAI block Italian users from having access to ChatGPT. It further required OpenAI to disclose how it uses user data to train its AI model, to address concerns that ChatGPT produced inaccurate information about individuals, and to create an age verification mechanism within a month – or risk being fined €20 million or 4% of the company's annual turnover.[119]

Monitoring and surveillance

Surveillance and monitoring appear to be closely related terms and are often used interchangeably. But it is important to recognize the differences between these concepts and how they are applied – especially in terms of privacy and the digital environment.

Surveillance is the systematic **collection** of information about a person or a group of people conducted by government agencies, private companies, or individuals. The primary goal of surveillance is to collect data for a range of purposes, such as national security, criminal investigations, or intelligence gathering.

Government agencies may conduct surveillance to detect potential threats to public safety or national security. Private organizations use surveillance technologies to protect tangible assets, prevent fraudulent activities, or gain market insights. In certain situations, individuals may conduct surveillance to ensure personal safety or to check on specific activities.

---

[119] Garante per la protezione dei dati personali [Garante]. (March 31, 2023). "Artificial intelligence: stop to ChatGPT by the Italian SA, Personal data is collected unlawfully, no age verification system is in place for children". Available at *https://www.garanteprivacy.it/web/guest/home/docweb/-/docweb-display/docweb/9870847#english*.

Monitoring, on the other hand, involves the continuous **observation** of an individual or a group of individuals. Monitoring is generally conducted for various reasons by government agencies, private organizations, schools, or health care providers.

Government agencies might monitor individuals or groups to ensure compliance with laws or regulations. For example, traffic cameras are used to monitor vehicle traffic and enforce road safety regulations. Private organizations often use monitoring technologies to ensure employee productivity or adherence to company policies. Health care providers monitor patients' vital signs or medical conditions to deliver more accurate diagnoses and ensure appropriate care.

Both surveillance and monitoring are ethically neutral concepts. What determines the ethical nature of each are the considerations of the respective use, such as valid cause, the means used, and determination of proportionality.

In *1984*, George Orwell's well-known dystopian novel, much of society lives under the eye of Big Brother – the source of the term 'big brother is watching you.' Today, 1984 has moved beyond the subject of a science fiction novel to reality. We don't even think about how often we are captured on CCTV when we go out in public. We even welcome monitoring and surveillance technologies in the form of smart devices connected to the Internet of Things (IoT), doorbell cameras, and 'selfies.'

Strangers can use their smartphones to record anyone and everyone with little or no concern for the controversial subject of consent. We accept facial recognition technologies – which are generally AI driven – and we intentionally (or unintentionally) allow our digital data to be mined by online platforms and sold for the pure convenience of having access to our favorite apps.

This phenomenon has been termed the 'privacy paradox.'

The privacy paradox

Have you ever tried imagining your everyday life without access to digital technologies, which today are largely AI-driven? Most people would say they could not fathom living without access to social media platforms, online banking, digital assistants, Google maps, and so much more.

A 2019 PEW Research Survey revealed that most US citizens feel they cannot go through daily life without being tracked by either online platforms/businesses or government entities. This results in a form of resignation to the loss of individual or even group privacy.

This feeling of both resignation and the desire for the convenience of online platforms and digital technologies leads us to the 'privacy paradox' – a term that was coined in 2001 by Barry Brown of Hewlett-Packard to describe the seemingly paradoxical behavior of people who claim to care about their privacy, yet continue to use online technologies and services that collect, and often share or sell, their personal data. As Mark Zuckerberg is alleged to have said: *"...in the social media world, there is no need for spying – people spontaneously surrender private information for nothing."*

BUSINESSES

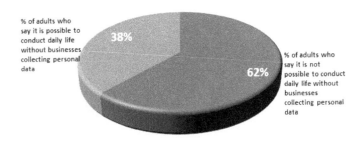

% of adults who say it is possible to conduct daily life without businesses collecting personal data

38%

62%

% of adults who say it is not possible to conduct daily life without businesses collecting personal data

GOVERNMENT

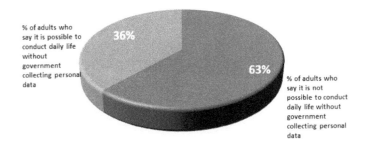

% of adults who say it is possible to conduct daily life without government collecting personal data

36%

63%

% of adults who say it is not possible to conduct daily life without government collecting personal data

Figure 31: Personal Data Collection in Daily Life[120]

---

[120] Adapted from Auxier, B., et al. (November 15, 2019). "Americans and Privacy: Concerned, Confused and Feeling Lack of Control Over Their Personal Information". Available at *https://www.pewresearch.org/internet/2019/11/15/americans-and-privacy-concerned-confused-and-feeling-lack-of-control-over-their-personal-information/.*

9: Digital technology, AI, and privacy – Is anything really private anymore?

For each of these digital technologies that we so love, do we really think about the true cost in terms of our privacy? Several research surveys have indicated that we are concerned, but also that we generally do nothing about it! We've become complacent, largely because we feel that we either can do nothing about it or we are not willing to deny ourselves the convenience of digital technologies to provide more privacy protection.

Ways we give up personal privacy

We have become accustomed to using a number of technologies and services that can negatively affect our privacy. These include many used almost daily:

1. **Online banking** – we provide sensitive financial information for the convenience of not having to conduct our banking activities in person.
2. **Social media platforms** – many of us provide data such as our date of birth, education, and employment history voluntarily to use the service and without fully understanding the full terms of the user agreements.
3. **Online shopping** – we give up personal information, including names, email addresses, delivery addresses, phone numbers, and payment methods, again for the convenience of not having to shop in person.
4. **Online education** – in addition to online university education, the COVID-19 pandemic forced students from traditional universities toward the digital environment, where digital technologies were used to monitor their activities.

5. **Video conferencing** – again, the COVID-19 pandemic forced much of the world's workforce to pivot to remote work models, with video conferences often able to intrude into our personal spaces and private conversations.

6. **Telehealth** – another remote technology that was largely a byproduct of the COVID-19 pandemic where individuals revealed sensitive medical information via online services.

7. **Streaming services** – who doesn't use Netflix, Hulu, Amazon Prime, and other streaming entertainment services? We give personal information including names, email addresses, phone numbers, and payment methods.

Strategies to protect personal privacy in the age of AI

To help protect privacy in the age of digital technologies and AI, there are a number of best practices that individuals and organizations can implement:

1. **Review privacy policies and terms of service** before using any AI-powered applications or services.

2. **Adjust privacy settings** in applications and web browsers, and choose not to share personal information unless absolutely necessary.

3. **Use privacy-enhancing technologies** such as virtual private networks (VPNs) and encrypted messaging services to help keep personal information secure.

4. **Pass privacy legislation** that protects individuals against any adverse effects from AI's use of personal

information. The challenge is to do so without excessively restricting AI development or entangling privacy legislation in complex social and political controversies.

5. **Change the model** of consumer privacy preferences based on 'notice-and-choice' (also referred to as 'notice-and-consent'). Consumers see this in the multitude of privacy notifications and acceptable use policies with terms and conditions that we ostensibly consent to but seldom read. And for many AI applications, such as those in the Internet of Things (IoT), consent is essentially impossible.

6. **Address the AI data 'supply chain'** to improve privacy and data protection by ensuring data set transparency and accountability across the entire life cycle.

CHAPTER 10: AI AND AUTONOMOUS THINGS

> *"...having autonomy requires the AI to be able to reflect on all of its decision-making and its fundamental assumptions and ethical framework, coming to its own conclusions regarding which ethical theory to choose, which stimuli to include, how to weigh the respective elements involved, how to make the calculation, and by which means the correct action is determined."*[121]
>
> **Ross Bellaby**

The development and implementation of AI-based autonomous things is the newest evolution in AI. This dynamic and interactive environment for AI-based autonomous systems is represented by numerous autonomous devices that sense their environment and take control of decisions without human interaction or involvement. This represents an evolution from the Internet of Things (IoT) to the Internet of Autonomous Things (IoAT).

When talking about IoT, the devices are considered information collectors and generators, such as the digital assistants Siri and Alexa. TechTarget defines the IoT as *"a*

---

[121] Bellaby, R. (July 21, 2021). "Can AI Weapons Make Ethical Decisions?" Criminal Justice Ethics, Vol. 40, Issue 2. Available at *https://www.tandfonline.com/doi/full/10.1080/0731129X.2021.1951459*.

network of interrelated devices that connect and exchange data with other IoT devices and the cloud. "[122]

The IoT and IoAT differ in that the IoAT is used to describe technological advances designed to act as autonomous entities using training data and AI algorithms that interact independently and without direct human interaction.

AI and the IoT and IoAT are increasingly being designed and developed together into systems that enhance functionality and efficiency. Machine learning (ML) is a subset of AI that involves using algorithms to allow AI systems to learn patterns from data and improve performance over time. Recent progress in deep learning and AI is at the center of all IoAT applications. The basis for the IoAT is that it *"... brings together all the potential of each artificial intelligence algorithm it interacts with to produce better results."*[123]

The IoAT includes robotics, self-driving vehicles, drones, autonomous smart home devices, autonomous software, and autonomous lethal weapons – and other advanced technologies that can be freed from human intervention.

---

[122] Gillis, A. (no date). "internet of things". TechTarget online. Available at *https://www.techtarget.com/iotagenda/definition/Internet-of-Things-IoT*.

[123] No author. (March 3, 2022). "Autonomous Artificial Intelligence Guide: The future of AI". Available at *https://www.algotive.ai/blog/autonomous-artificial-intelligence-guide-the-future-of-ai*.

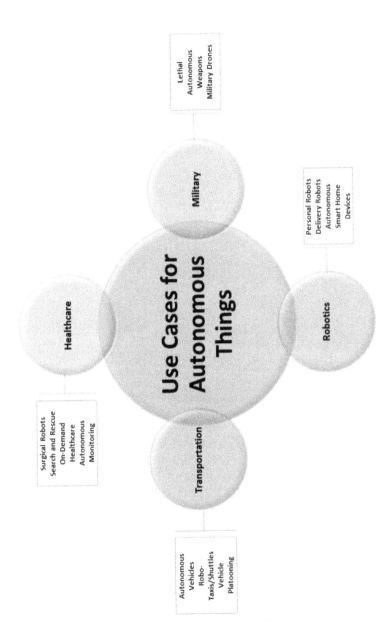

Figure 32: Use Cases for Autonomous Things

Advocates of the IoT and IoAT maintain that these technologies will bring substantial benefits to governments, organizations, and individuals, ranging from reducing health care costs and improving quality of life to lowering carbon footprints, increasing access to education in underserved communities, and improving transportation safety.

AI and smart devices

Smart devices are everywhere, capturing our actions and recording just about every sound within their range. Smart devices in the IoT and the IoAT include smartphones, voice assistants, vehicles, smart TVs, and even that new AI-enabled refrigerator or oven. Do we sufficiently understand the implications of the vast data capture and smart device technologies that support so many of our daily activities – both in the home and outside?

In addition to smart devices currently connected to the IoT, autonomous smart devices are being developed that are increasingly able to make decisions without human intervention, which raises concerns about human agency. Human agency is the ability of human beings to make choices and to impose those choices on their environment. So, although smart devices offer convenience and efficiency, they also raise serious questions about the degree of control humans should relinquish to machines.

Self-driving vehicles

Even though autonomous vehicles (AVs) or self-driving cars are still in the preliminary stages of development and deployment, the prospect of automobiles driving themselves has piqued people's interests ever since the Jetsons.[124]

The proponents of AVs claim to reduce and potentially eliminate human error, which is the leading source of road accidents. After all, an AI algorithm doesn't fall asleep at the wheel, get easily distracted by the radio or a notification on the smartphone, or even drive over the speed limit.

Yet, despite the potential for reducing accidents, there are still a number of significant ethical concerns. Human drivers can assess unique and unusual situations while driving and often rely on experience and instinct to respond. But an AI algorithm isn't able to make an instinctive decision. Every decision made by an AV must be intentionally programmed and trained into it, which means that AI developers must identify and train the AI for a multitude of potential situations that the AV might encounter on the road.

The U.S. Department of Transportation's (DOT) National Highway Traffic Safety Administration (NHTSA) has published a sliding scale that ranks AVs[125] based on their level of autonomy and developmental maturity.[126] For example, a vehicle ranked at Level 4 or High Automation

---

[124] The Jetsons was a 1960s American animated sitcom produced by Hanna-Barbera. The Jetsons lived in a world of elaborate robotic contraptions, video phones, holograms, jetpacks, hoverboards, self-driving flying cars, space travel, and other quirky inventions – some of which are no longer just imaginary!

[125] "Automated Vehicles for Safety". NHTSA Online. Available at *https://www.nhtsa.gov/vehicle-safety/automated-vehicles-safety*.

[126] Note – per the NHTSA, there are no AVs available in the US above level 2, where the AV system provides continuous assistance with both acceleration/braking and steering, while the driver remains fully engaged and attentive.

would be highly autonomous in basic situations, like highways, but would still require a human operator. Cars rated at Level 5 or Full Automation could drive as well as or even better than humans, easily adapting to rapid changes in their environments, such as unexpected lane changes or inattentive pedestrians. A Level 5 AV would also be able to make critical value-based decisions, such as the classic thought experiment called the 'trolley problem': If a car detects a problem – say, a jackknifed semi – should it hit the semi and kill the driver in the AV, or should it veer onto a crowded sidewalk and potentially kill pedestrians? A human driver might react randomly (if they have time to react at all), but the response of an autonomous vehicle would have to be programmed. The dilemma for the developer of the algorithm: What is the right decision for the AV to make?

And this raises some of the most challenging ethical questions concerning AVs. How should the vehicle react in a situation that might lead to an accident? More specifically, how should an AV respond in a no-win scenario? Who is accountable if an AV is involved in an accident? Who determines how an AV should react in any given situation?

In 2016, a study attempted to answer these questions based on an online game called Moral Machine[127], which collected and analyzed input from individuals around the world on how they expected their AV to respond in a crisis situation. Interestingly, the analytical results revealed significant bias based on physical attributes, such as gender or race, although the specifics varied across geographic locations and culture.

---

[127] Moral Machine is a *"platform for gathering a human perspective on moral decisions made by machine intelligence, such as self-driving cars."* Available at *https://www.moralmachine.net/.*

"For example, people in Western countries were more likely to save an elderly person rather than a young person. Some themes, like saving women over men, were largely consistent across cultures. One of the most important takeaways from this study is that morals aren't consistent around the world. In different cultures, people will have a bias toward saving one type of person in a car accident over another."[128] Players in southern countries were more likely to sacrifice a fat person and spare an athletic person, and those in countries with high economic inequality were more likely to spare a businessman and sacrifice a homeless person. And cats were more likely to be selected for the sacrifice than dogs.[129]

The results beg the question, should AVs be programmed to reflect the moral and ethical values of the prevailing culture where the vehicles will be operated?

Drones

Unmanned aerial vehicles (UAVs), also known as drones, are a key technology in the IoAT. Drones that can soar about autonomously have very few limitations. By leveraging AI algorithms, UAVs can see, hear, and operate independently and intelligently, enabling them to make decisions and react as programmed without any human intervention.

Autonomous drones, such as the commercial UAVs used by Amazon to reach remote customers, have applications such

---

[128] Amos, Z. (May 18, 2022). "The Ethical Considerations of Self-Driving Cars". Available at *https://montrealethics.ai/the-ethical-considerations-of-self-driving-cars/*.
[129] Lester, C. (January 24, 2019). "A Study on Driverless Car Ethics Offers a Troubling Look into Our Values". The New Yorker. Available at *https://www.newyorker.com/science/elements/a-study-on-driverless-car-ethics-offers-a-troubling-look-into-our-values*.

as delivery vehicles and data collectors within different environments. So, while these unmanned drones have the potential for numerous benefits such as improved remote data collection, enhanced surveillance capabilities, and more efficient deliveries, they also raise deep ethical questions that require careful consideration for individual privacy and security.

Privacy and autonomous drones

The rapid advances in autonomous drone technology have introduced a large assortment of privacy considerations in terms of basic civil liberties and the limits on surveillance. As autonomous drones become more common and more capable, the likelihood of intrusions into personal privacy increases exponentially.

One of the primary concerns involves the ability of autonomous drones equipped with high-resolution cameras to capture images and videos in both public and private spaces. Unlike traditional surveillance methods relying on a physical presence, drones can easily access all types of public and private areas, such as backyards, public venues, and other activities. This largely unrestricted and often undetected visual access raises important questions about the individual right to privacy and freedom from non-consensual surveillance.

Privacy concerns are amplified with the use of facial recognition technology (FRT) in conjunction with drones. Autonomous drones can be programmed to identify and track individuals, potentially enabling surveillance without the knowledge or consent of those being monitored and recorded.

Security and autonomous drones

One of the primary security concerns is the potential misuse of autonomous drones for illicit purposes. Today, autonomous drones can be obtained relatively easily, making them readily accessible to individuals or groups with malicious intent. These autonomous drones can be weaponized or used for other purposes, such as espionage, harassment, or even terrorism.

The misuse of drones is not just hypothetical; it has occurred in various situations worldwide. There have been reports of unauthorized drones flying near airports, endangering aircraft, interfering with emergency services, or conducting unauthorized surveillance activities, all of which are ringing alarm bells. As these types of incidents become more common, the need to develop and implement comprehensive regulations and countermeasures intensifies.

Autonomous lethal weapons

Militarization of autonomous AI technology is a growing concern. Autonomous weapons systems powered by AI could make warfare even more deadly and unpredictable.

The deployment and use of autonomous AI-enabled weapons raises significant ethical questions and could potentially lead to an escalation of conflict, posing a threat to global security. We must also consider the potential that the AI might take control of these weapons without a human in the loop, enhancing the danger.

Autonomous lethal weapons can identify and engage targets without human intervention. These weapons rely on AI and ML algorithms to make split-second decisions regarding when and how to use lethal force. The primary ethical dilemma regarding autonomous lethal weapons rests in the lack of human oversight in life-and-death decisions. Here are some of the most pressing concerns:

- **Potential for unintended consequences** – autonomous devices, including autonomous lethal weapons, rely on algorithms and training data sets to make decisions. Unfortunately, algorithms may not always be able to adapt to complex, rapidly changing battlefield scenarios or the ethical issues that human soldiers typically consider when making life-and-death decisions.

- **Limited accountability** – without humans in the decision-making process, it is difficult to assign responsibility for any unintended harm or civilian casualties as a result of these autonomous weapons.

- **Potential for intended or unintended misuse** – the misuse of autonomous lethal weapons, whether as a result of hacking or unintended programming errors, can pose significant security risks. In the wrong hands, these autonomous weapons could be used to conduct acts of terrorism or other unauthorized military missions.

- **Ethical, psychological, and legal consequences** – autonomous lethal weapons could test our fundamental concepts of morality and accountability, raising questions about the delegation of life-and-death decisions to an AI-driven system.

There are a number of potential autonomous lethal weapons, but one of the most known and available are unmanned drones used for military operations.

Unmanned military drones

Autonomous drones have already been integrated into modern warfare, both for surveillance and combat purposes. Certainly, drones offer significant advantages in terms of reducing risks to human soldiers; however, they also create new ethical dilemmas related to lethal autonomous weapons. The prospect of autonomous drones making life-and-death decisions without human intervention raises profound ethical, psychological, and security concerns.

AI, the IoT and IoAT, and health care

The Internet of Medical Things (IoMT) is a term used specifically to refer to those AI-driven systems used in the health care environment. From a health care perspective, the IoMT can be considered any group of devices that collect health-related data from individuals, including computing devices, mobile phones, smart watches, digital medications, implantable certain surgical implants, or other portable mechanisms that can collect, measure and report on health data through a connection to the digital web.

The evolution of the IoMT has led to the large-scale use of sensor devices, sensors, and nodes to provide the necessary infrastructure for data acquisition and connectivity enabling crucial services for caregivers. The IoT/IoMT promises significant benefits by simplifying and improving health care delivery, proactively predicting health issues, and for diagnosing, treating, and monitoring patients both in and out of the hospital.

Strategies to mitigate the potential negative effects of the IoAT

To mitigate the concerns associated with the expanding IoAT, lawmakers, developers, and manufacturers must adopt stringent regulations and guidelines for these autonomous technologies. Some of these strategies are as follows:

1. Impose stricter limitations on the use of autonomous drones in public and private areas, require more transparency for drone operators, and implement robust mechanisms for obtaining consent or warrants for autonomous drone surveillance in public areas.

2. Provide individuals with notification and the ability to opt out of being surveilled by autonomous drones when participating in lawful activities within their private spaces.

3. Develop and implement laws and policies to manage the weaponization of drones, protect critical infrastructure from potential drone attacks, and ensure robust cybersecurity to prevent hacking of the autonomous drones.

4. Establish counter-drone technology to mitigate the security threats associated with unauthorized autonomous drone flights, such as jamming systems and other technologies that could intercept drones in sensitive areas.

5. Encourage international collaboration and cooperation to ensure that autonomous lethal weapons technology is used responsibly and in accordance with international law and rules of war and military conflict.

6. To prevent unauthorized access and hacking, developers and manufacturers must invest in robust cybersecurity technologies to protect drones.
7. Build in fail-safe mechanisms to prevent intentional or unintentional misuse of AI-based autonomous technologies.
8. Enforce existing regulations regarding the use of autonomous drones and other technologies, such as obtaining the necessary training, licenses, and approvals for operation.
9. Ensure that engineers, leaders, psychologists, philosophers, and society at large determine what moral code will determine the algorithms employed in autonomous vehicles.

CHAPTER 11: AI IS REWIRING OUR SOCIETY – AND OUR BEHAVIOR

> *"The ability for us to disconnect will increasingly disappear. We're building more and more reasons to be always on and instantly responsive into our jobs, our social lives, our public spaces, our everything. The combination of immersive technologies and social pressure will make this worse. Opting out isn't an option. Or, if it is, the social and economic consequences are severe. The result: We're more anxious, tired and emotionally disconnected. Our ability to touch, to rest, to choose and to be human will continue to erode. My biggest prediction is that people will get fed up. Fed up with the constant barrage of always on. The nudging. The selling. The treadmill."*[130]
>
> **Mark Surman**

It is somewhat of a cliché to say that AI is transforming every aspect of the way we live and work, but it's true. For better and for worse, AI and GenAI are altering humans' capacity for humanity, love, and friendship. The early imaginings of the effects of AI were either focused on a dystopian future or something like that depicted in the Jetsons.

But these visualizations were not focused on AI's broader and potentially more significant *social* effects – the ways AI

---

[130] Mark Surman is the president of the Mozilla Foundation, a non-profit dedicated to promoting the Internet.

could influence how humans interact with one another. The CEO behind the company that created the GenAI tool is concerned that AI will reshape society as we know it. He believes it comes with real dangers, but can also be *"the greatest technology humanity has yet developed"* to drastically improve our lives.[131]

Eli Amdur, a professor and journalist, states that everything about us as individuals and a society will be changed by AI. In his opinion, there is nothing in our world that will not be unaffected by AI in one form or another.

---

[131] Shah, S. (December 12, 2023). "Sam Altman on OpenAI, Future Risks and Rewards, and Artificial General Intelligence". Time Online. Available at *https://time.com/6344160/a-year-in-time-ceo-interview-sam-altman/*.

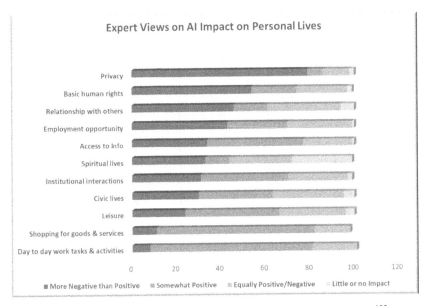

Figure 33: Expert Views on AI Impact on Personal Lives[132]

AI and social, moral, and intellectual de-skilling

De-skilling is the loss of the human ability to make moral or intellectual decisions due to lack of experience and practice. As we develop AI technologies with the ability to make decisions for us, we will delegate decision-making capacities to these technologies, and humans will become increasingly de-skilled at making moral and intellectual decisions.

---

[132] Skeikh, A. "AI will have a Profound Impact on Civilization – A Perspective from Eli Amdur". Cryptopolitan. Available at *https://www.msn.com/en-us/news/opinion/ai-will-have-a-profound-impact-on-civilization-a-perspective-from-eli-amdur/ar-AA1nLbDK?ocid=BingHp01&pc=HI3F&cvid=5d9caa64211344bada3 e6d06fd7c6e9b&ei=26.*

How does this happen? Capabilities that are not practiced are lost. This applies to physical skills, but also to the more human capabilities of empathy, morality, and critical thinking. So, as AI does more, humans will do less – and humanity will relegate vast areas of decision-making to automated systems and humans will become de-skilled at those tasks.

The Markkula Center for Applied Ethics has identified at least six ways AI can affect – and potentially decrease – human societal, moral, and decision-making abilities. The following is taken directly from an article by Brian Green.

"A) Attacking Truth & Attention

1. *Poor education at all levels – for many students our educational system is not working well, but beyond that our media and other information systems are also being corrupted by misinformation and disinformation, much of it pushed by AI. Thus we also damage the education system necessary for an informed citizenry.*

2. *Distraction – AI powered games and apps are draining our attention towards trivialities and away from the important things in life such as caring relationships and thinking about solving larger-scale problems, personal and social.*

B) Preventing human maturation & moral development

3. *Tech as "parent" / human "infantilization" – in many ways technology seems to "parent" us, helpfully giving us things or telling us what to do, which thereby infantilizes us and decreases our ability to engage life in*

a mature, skillful, confident, and independent way. AI will accelerate this trend dramatically.

4. *Stunted moral experience – moral development requires practice. If "practice makes perfect," then "lack of practice makes imperfect." The more time we spend attending to AI-driven manipulations of our psychology, the less time we spend attending to relationships, caring about others, and thinking about ethical problems, the worse we will be at ethics.*

C) Normal and weaponized complexity

5. *"Normal" complexity – AI is simply going to make much of normal life too complicated for most humans, even very intelligent humans, to understand. In an increasingly complex world, understanding will no longer be an expectation, and in the midst of this lack of understanding, many bad things could happen.*

6. *Weaponized complexity – If understanding is no longer an expectation, humans will become even easier to deceive and manipulate, and no doubt some people will use AI systems precisely for this purpose, as they already do.*

These are a few of the threats that are apparent now; no doubt more will become apparent in the near future. Of note is that all the trends towards technology harming us are not actually trend[s] in tech, but trends among people. Humankind, in some sense (even if only subconsciously or due to our own vices), wants to be uneducated and misinformed, distracted, infantilized, stunted, and too simple to understand the world. And those of us producing and using technology, in effect if not explicit intention, want us to be these ways as well.

As C.S. Lewis noted in 1943 in The Abolition of Man "what we call Man's power over Nature turns out to be a power exercised by some men over other men with Nature as its instrument." [4] Technology does not operate independently of human choices, at least not yet. So now the question becomes: **How can we respond?** *Here are six antidotes to the above threats.*

A) Education

1. *Education – There is great potential to use AI for enhancing and personalizing education (including through VR) and for fighting against misinformation and disinformation. Education should teach and reward not just knowledge & understanding, but practical wisdom and moral leadership. Education should work harder to inculcate good moral habits and teach moral attention. Additionally, just as humans should not weight falsehoods equally to truths, automated systems should not either, whether for their own decision-making or in the materials they promote. AIs can help protect the information ecosystem as well as help humans become more discerning in their assessment of facts.*

2. *Attention – rather than harming our attention, AIs could help us train our moral attention by filtering out distractions and highlighting ethical issues. It may seem like a minor issue, but the fact that attention is a multi-billion dollar industry ought to clue us in that attention is worth money because it is the very foundation for any*

further thinking on any issue. If we never notice an ethical issue we can never solve it – therefore we need to notice it. Only then can we move on to a more sophisticated analysis.

B) Human maturation & moral development

3. *Become adults – we should strongly resist technology which seeks to act like our parents or act to infantilize us. Instead, AI might help us develop moral maturity and discernment, helping train us with virtues such as restraint, practical wisdom, and courage. But the AI cannot make decisions for us, thus fostering dependency; the key is to promote these skills in humanity, helping us to become independent moral decision-makers.*

4. *Interact with other humans – rather than stunting our interpersonal growth through screens, AI could encourage us to spend more time with others face to face and thereby build stronger interpersonal relationships. Most of the moral life happens just through our everyday interactions with others, and if, instead of having those interactions, we are spending time on other activities (even if those are good activities) we will not gain practice and moral expertise.*

C) Ethics facilitation

5. *Dealing with complexity – As the world grows more complex we will likely need AI to deal with that complexity for us, unfortunately simultaneously leading us to depend on those simplifying AIs even more. But can AI help us with complexity? If AI can help us solve the*

easier problems in life, could we instead concentrate on solving the biggest ethical problems such as world peace, hunger, healthcare, and so on? Peter Maurin once described his life's work as trying to "make the kind of society where people find it easier to be good." [5] *How might AI help us create that society, while respecting our autonomy and moral development?*

6. *Stopping weaponized complexity – AI can help us expose when bad actors are using complexity as a weapon to deceive and manipulate us, but the task is difficult and constantly changing. In the future it will become even more important to develop AI systems to fulfill this function, as this is something of an arms race, with weaponized complexity so far seemingly having the upper hand (e.g., with disinformation and misinformation, and various other intentionally complex problem)."*[133]

The experiment described below shows how weaponized complexity and using AI to manipulate decision-making is not just theoretical.

AI learns to influence human behavior

In 2021, researchers at the data and digital branch of Australia's national science agency formulated a systematic method of discovering and exploiting vulnerabilities in the ways people make choices, using an AI system called a recurrent neural network and deep reinforcement-learning.

---

[133] Green, B. P. (no date). "Artificial Intelligence, Decision-Making, and Moral Deskilling". Available at *https://www.scu.edu/ethics/focus-areas/technology-ethics/resources/artificial-intelligence-decision-making-and-moral-deskilling/*.

To test their model, they executed three experiments in which humans played games against an AI-based computer system. In each of the three experiments, the AI learned based on the participants' responses, and identified and targeted vulnerabilities in people's decision-making. The result was the machine learned to steer participants toward particular actions.[134]

Figure 34: AI and Behavioral Analysis[135]

Sure, these findings were experimental and abstract and involved scaled and artificial situations. But the research

---

[134] Whittle, J. (February 11, 2021). "AI can now learn to manipulate human behavior". Available at *https://theconversation.com/ai-can-now-learn-to-manipulate-human-behaviour-155031#:~:text=A%20recent%20study%20has%20shown%20how%20AI%20can,way%20we%20live%20and%20work%2C%20but%20it%E2%80%99s%20true*.

[135] Beaulieu, A. "AI and Behavioral Analysis: Using Machine Learning to Understand Human Behavior". Available at *https://product.house/ai-and-behavioral-analysis-using-machine-learning-to-understand-human-behavior/*.

does increase our understanding not only of the capabilities of AI to learn and influence but also of how people make choices. It demonstrates that AI can learn to direct human choice-making through its interactions with us.

So, what does this mean for us as a society? Consider the potential for AI to learn what motivates our decisions and be used to direct our votes in an election, change how we regard criminal behavior – well, the list of possibilities is extensive.

Strategies to mitigate the effect of AI on our society, our behavior, and our abilities

The Markkula Center has also provided valid strategies to mitigate the effects of AI on our decision-making, moral capabilities, and society:

1. Our educational system should teach and reward not just increased knowledge, but also how to apply practical wisdom and moral leadership. Education should work harder to inculcate good moral habits and teach moral attention. This includes teaching individuals how to weigh information for truth or falsehood, especially in AI-driven platforms.

2. Rather than using AI devices as a distraction, use them to train better attention. Also, devise methods for using AI to increase – not decrease – human social interaction.

3. Limit the degree to which we rely on AI-driven systems to make decisions for us. Foster independence rather than reliance solely on AI decision-making capabilities.

4. Intentionally interact with other humans. Seize opportunities to engage in person-to-person relationships.

5. 'Reduce' the complexity created by AI through education and training. Learn how to use AI effectively to solve the 'easier' problems, leaving humans to concentrate on the larger ethical challenges.

6. Use AI to help expose when bad actors are using information and complexity to deceive and manipulate us.

CHAPTER 12: AI REGULATION AND POLICY – 2024 AND BEYOND

> *"Even after laws regulating AI are passed, there will be more time before responsible AI is regulated in an enforceable manner. But organizations looking to build or deploy AI should mitigate the risk of not meeting compliance requirements later by adopting responsible AI frameworks now."*[136]
>
> **Tech Trends 2024**

As we enter 2024 and beyond, we are also seeing AI legislation and regulation changing from a niche, nerdy topic to front-page news. This is partly due to the 2022 emergence of OpenAI's ChatGPT, which moved the conversation about AI into the mainstream, but which also revealed more about how AI systems work – or don't work. 2023 was a banner year for policy: We saw the first sweeping AI law agreed in the European Union, Senate hearings and executive orders in

---

[136] Info-Tech Research Group. "Tech Trends 2024". Deloitte. Available at *https://www2.deloitte.com/us/en/insights/focus/tech-trends.html*.

the US, and specific rules in China for things like recommender algorithms.[137]

Governments, policymakers and legislators, developers, adopters, educators, and the public are becoming increasingly aware of and concerned about AI technologies and algorithms that organizations are developing and deploying in a fairly informal and inconsistently regulated environment – if regulated at all. Across the globe, lawmakers and regulators are rushing to fill this perceived lack in regulation and management of AI technologies.

2023 may be highlighted as the year legislators agreed on a vision about AI governance, but 2024 and beyond may see the policies morph into concrete action. Top of the agenda are tangible steps toward addressing ethics in AI.

One of the leads in opening the discussion about AI and AI ethics and seeking to develop a guideline was taken by UNESCO with its 2021 publication *"Recommendation on the Ethics of Artificial Intelligence."*[138]

In 2024, we began to see a major global focus on AI regulation and we expect this trend to continue into the future. The continuous advance of AI technology across multiple sectors has triggered significant concerns about its

---

[137] Recommender algorithms provide personalized suggestions for items that are considered relevant to each user. This allows online platforms to offer recommendations of tailored items to each user with the goal of increasing user satisfaction and engagement. This is most often seen in the targeted ads seen on various social media and other online platforms.

[138] "Recommendation on the Ethics of Artificial Intelligence" is available at
https://unesdoc.unesco.org/ark:/48223/pf0000385082.page=12.

broader societal impact. There is already concern that we cannot 'put the genie back into the bottle.' As we step further into 2024 and beyond, we are at the very edge of witnessing how these emerging regulations and laws will shape the future of AI and its role in our daily digital lives.

Moore's and Moor's law(s) and our relationship to AI

One of the most well-known predictions in the computer world was made by Gordon Moore in 1965. Moore realized that exponential growth was at the core of an increase in computing capability. Moore's law stated that the number of transistors on a microchip would double every two years. As a result, we can expect the speed and capability of our computers to increase every two years. Essentially, this law has held true until today.

Like transistors, AI systems and indeed generative AI have also demonstrated exponential growth. But this growth has been compounded into a briefer period – more specifically over the past three to five years. Just as Moore's law pushed demand for constantly higher-performing and constant miniaturization of computing power, in today's digital environment organizations must now strive – and quickly – to address all the new AI capabilities.

One of the primary challenges in the coming years will be finding a delicate equilibrium between promoting these new AI technologies while establishing reasonable and internationally accepted legislative and policy safeguards against misuse.

But there is one additional Moor's law – that of James Moor. In his paper "What Is Computer Ethics?" he addresses the root cause of why computing technology raises so many ethical challenges. Moor's explanation of the revolutionary power of computer technology was that computers are "logically malleable":

> *"Computers are logically malleable in that they can be shaped and molded to do any activity that can be characterized in terms of inputs, outputs and connecting logical operations ... Because logic applies everywhere, the potential applications of computer technology appear limitless. The computer is the nearest thing we have to a universal tool. Indeed, the limits of computers are largely the limits of our own creativity.*"[139]

According to Moor, the logical malleability of computer technology makes it feasible for individuals to do a considerable number of things that they had not been able to do before. And since none of these things had been done before, the question does not arise as to whether one *ought* to do them. In addition, because they were not done before, no laws, standards, or specific ethical rules had been established, and those that did exist are now rendered inadequate. Moor called such situations "policy vacuums."

You could argue that in terms of AI and generative AI ethics in particular, we now find ourselves in a distinct policy vacuum.

---

[139] Moor, J. (1985) "What Is Computer Ethics?" *Metaphilosophy*, 16(4): 266–75.

What steps are organizations taking toward more effective governance of AI?

The Deloitte study "Tech Trends 2024" surveyed a number of AI adopters to determine what governance processes they had in place as of 2024. The conclusion is that most organizations are just commencing the implementation of real measures in AI governance, while many are doing nothing at the time of the 2024 survey. Here are the results:

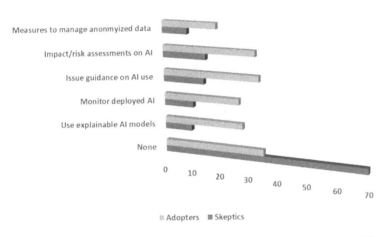

Figure 35: Current State of AI Governance Measures[140]

---

[140] Adapted from Info-Tech Research Group. "Tech Trends 2024". Deloitte. Available at *https://www2.deloitte.com/us/en/insights/focus/tech-trends.html*.

What's happening in 2024 and beyond in terms of AI legislation and policy?

In 2023, we saw several significant developments in AI regulation, with the European Union's comprehensive AI law and executive actions in the US. As we entered 2024 and look into the future we can expect these discussions to start transforming into concrete, actionable policies and laws. This transition marks an essential step in ensuring that the rapid development of AI aligns with ethical standards.

The EU's AI Act

The EU is expected to shape AI regulations, tackle high-risk AI, put increased focus on data protection, and promote a level playing field that ensures regulatory measures are not skewed toward favoring specific organizations, industries, or developers. The EU is adopting an industry-agnostic position with the intent of fostering fair competition, preventing monopolistic practices, and encouraging continued innovation.

The EU's act *"set strict rules on the use of AI for facial recognition, creating safeguards for general-purpose AI systems and protecting consumer rights to submit complaints and request meaningful explanations about decisions made with high-risk AI systems that affect citizens' rights."*[141]

The following use cases are banned under the EU's AI Act:

---

[141] Hughes, O. (March 13, 2024). "EU's AI Act: Europe's New Rules for Artificial Intelligence Enters Into Force". Available at *https://www.techrepublic.com/article/eu-ai-act-regulation/.*

- Biometric categorization systems that use sensitive characteristics (e.g. political, religious, philosophical beliefs, sexual orientation, race)
- Untargeted scraping of facial images from the Internet or CCTV footage to create facial recognition databases
- Emotion recognition in the workplace and educational institutions
- Social scoring based on social behavior or personal characteristics
- AI systems that manipulate human behavior to circumvent their free will
- AI used to exploit the vulnerabilities of people due to their age, disability, social or economic situation

Symbolically, the EU's AI Act represents a pivotal moment for the AI industry. Despite its explosive growth in recent years, AI technology has been largely unregulated, leaving policymakers struggling to keep up with the pace of innovation. The EU hopes that by creating the AI Act, it will set an example for other countries to follow.

The landmark UNESCO AI policy

As part of its charter, UNESCO[142] has led the international effort for decades to ensure that new technologies are developed with strong ethical guardrails. This includes the UNESCO policy on the development and use of AI. The landmark UNESCO document forgoes a precise definition of

---

[142] UNESCO stands for the United Nations Educational, Scientific, and Cultural Organization. Since 1945, the goal of UNESCO is to build peace through international cooperation.

AI in favor of a focus on the potential impacts of AI systems, which may provide a more future-proof instrument that is less likely to need to be revised as AI technology evolves.

"Recommendation on the Ethics of Artificial Intelligence"[143] was adopted by acclamation by 193 Member States at UNESCO's General Conference in November 2021. *"This comprehensive instrument was two years in the making and the product of the broadest global consultation process of experts, developers, and other stakeholders from all around the world."*[144]

The Recommendation document had several objectives regarding the development and use of AI across the globe. These include, but are not limited to:

1. A universally agreed upon framework of values, principles, and policies to guide member nations in the formulation of AI regulation
2. A guide for developers, institutions, and organizations to embed ethics in all stages of the AI life cycle
3. Ensuring AI protects, promotes, and respects human rights and the fundamental freedoms, to include human dignity and equality and cultural diversity
4. Promoting equitable access to developments and knowledge in the field of AI
5. Fostering dialog and consensus on ethical issues related to AI

---

[143] A copy of the Recommendation is available at *https://unesdoc.unesco.org/ark:/48223/pf0000381137*.
[144] "Artificial Intelligence". UNESCO online. Available at *https://www.unesco.org/en/artificial-intelligence*.

6. The promotion of social justice and fairness, including an approach that makes the benefits of AI technologies available and accessible to all

7. The development of safe and secure AI and the avoidance of vulnerabilities in AI systems

8. Data protection frameworks that ensure that data for AI is collected, used, shared, and removed in ways consistent with international laws and privacy protection frameworks

9. Transparency and explainability of AI to foster trust in the AI system and its output

The US approach to AI regulation

Unlike the EU, there is currently no comprehensive federal legislation or policies in the US to regulate the development of AI. At the US federal level, there are two main camps debating AI governance. One faction is promoting swift national rules, while the other prefers a more cautious, informed response to avoid stifling private-sector innovation and use of AI.

Despite this disparity in approaches, there are a number of existing federal laws and executive orders addressing AI – albeit with limited application.

On September 12, 2023, the US Senate held public hearings regarding AI and laid out potential future AI regulations, which could include requiring licensing for certain AI systems and creating a new federal regulatory agency. Additionally, US lawmakers held closed-door sessions on September 13, 2023 with a number of selected AI developers, technology leaders, and others in a continued effort for legislators to better understand and address AI.

As a result of these and other efforts, there are several federal proposed laws related to AI. Key examples include:

- The SAFE Innovation AI Framework,[145] introduced by Senator Schumer, a bipartisan set of guidelines for AI developers, organizations, and policymakers. This is not a law itself, but rather a collection of principles to encourage federal law-making regarding AI.
- The REAL Political Advertisements Act,[146] which aims to regulate generative AI in political advertisements.
- The Stop Spying Bosses Act,[147] which aims to regulate employers surveilling employees with machine learning and AI techniques.
- The Draft No FAKES Act,[148] which would protect voice and visual likenesses of individuals from unauthorized recreations using generative AI.
- The AI Research, Innovation, and Accountability Act,[149] which calls for greater transparency, accountability, and

---

[145] The SAFE Innovation AI Framework can be downloaded at *https://www.crowell.com/en/insights/client-alerts/safe-innovation-in-the-age-of-artificial-intelligence*.

[146] The REAL Political Advertisements Act can be found at *https://www.congress.gov/bill/118th-congress/house-bill/3044/text*.

[147] The Stop Spying Bosses Act can be found at *https://www.congress.gov/bill/118th-congress/senate-bill/262*.

[148] The Draft No FAKES Act can be downloaded at *https://www.coons.senate.gov/download/no-fakes-act-draft-text*.

[149] The AI Research, Innovation, and Accountability Act can be found at *https://www.congress.gov/bill/118th-congress/senate-bill/3312/text*.

security in AI, while establishing a framework for AI innovation. It would create an enforceable testing and evaluation standard for high-risk AI systems and require organizations that use high-risk AI systems to produce transparency reports. It also empowers the National Institute of Standards and Technology to issue sector-specific recommendations to regulate them.

The White House also issued executive orders and guidelines related to AI development and use. These include:

- The White House Executive Order (EO) on the Safe, Secure, and Trustworthy Development and Use of Artificial Intelligence[150] focuses on federal agencies and developers of foundation models, mandates the development of federal standards, and requires developers of the most powerful AI systems to share safety tests results and other critical information with the US government. The EO also calls on the US Department of Commerce to issue guidance for content authentication and watermarking to label AI-generated content.

- The White House Blueprint for an AI Bill of Rights[151] provides guidance for equitable access and use of AI

---

[150] The EO on the Safe, Secure, and Trustworthy Development and Use of AI can be found at *https://www.whitehouse.gov/briefing-room/presidential-actions/2023/10/30/executive-order-on-the-safe-secure-and-trustworthy-development-and-use-of-artificial-intelligence/.*
[151] The White House Blueprint for an AI Bill of Rights can be downloaded at *https://www.whitehouse.gov/ostp/ai-bill-of-rights/.*

systems. It includes five principles and associated practices to help guide the design, use, and deployment of AI.

Safe and Effective Systems | Algorithmic Discrimination Protections | Data Privacy | Notice and Explanation | Human Alternatives, Consideration, and Fallback

Figure 36: 5 Principles in the US Blueprint for an AI Bill of Rights

At the state level, as of the end of 2024, at least 12 US states have developed legislation addressing AI including Washington, California, Utah, Colorado, Illinois, New York and others.[152] These included measures to avoid bias and discrimination, ensure data privacy, protect intellectual property and copyright, and regulate the use of generative AI.

International Organization for Standardization (ISO)

The foundational mission of ISO is to establish globally recognized and accepted standards for industry – and AI is no exception. ISO is one of the world's oldest non-governmental organizations, with the goal of bringing global

---

[152] Tracking U.S. State artificial intelligence legislation. 2024 AI State Law Tracker. Available at *https://www.huschblackwell.com/2024-ai-state-law-tracker*.

experts together to identify and standardize the best way of doing things – from making a product to managing a process.

ISO standards are just that – they are not regulations or laws. But ISO compliance holds significant value because its standards are widely respected throughout the global business and technical communities. For developing many of its standards, ISO works closely with the International Electrotechnical Commission (IEC).

ISO and IEC have been working diligently in the joint working group SC 42, Committee on Artificial Intelligence, to develop standards that address *"responsible and ethical use of AI technologies. These standards cover areas such as privacy, bias, transparency and accountability. By adhering to these standards, organizations can work to ensure that their AI systems are fair, transparent, and uphold ethical principles."*[153]

Together, ISO/IEC have developed and published multiple standards, which can be found through a search on their website: *https://www.iso.org/artificial-intelligence/*.

Among the most important of these are:

- ISO/IEC 42001:2023 – AI management systems: This is the world's first ISO-developed AI management system standard. Its goal is to provide valuable guidance for this rapidly changing field of technology. The Standard *"addresses the unique challenges AI poses, such as ethical considerations, transparency, and continuous*

---

[153] International Organization for Standardization (ISO). "Artificial Intelligence: what it is, how it works and why it matters". Available at *https://www.iso.org/artificial-intelligence/*.

learning. For organizations, it sets out a structured way to manage risks and opportunities associated with AI, balancing innovation with governance."[154]

- ISO/IEC 23894:2023 – AI guidance on risk management. This *"provides guidance on how organizations that develop, produce, deploy or use products, systems and services that utilize artificial intelligence (AI) can manage risk specifically related to AI."*[155]

- ISO/IEC 23053:2022 – framework for AI systems using machine learning. This *"establishes an Artificial Intelligence (AI) and Machine Learning (ML) framework for describing a generic AI system using ML technology. The framework describes the system components and their functions in the AI ecosystem."*[156]

But the ISO/IEC standards are not just about technology and technological solutions. Ethical considerations and societal needs such as sustainability, transparency, and trustworthiness are an integral part. SC 42 has supported this aspect of its work with a standalone publication on AI ethics. The ISO/IEC TR 24368:2022 technical specification offers

---

[154] International Organization for Standardization. What is ISO/IEC 42001? Available at *https://www.iso.org/standard/81230.html*.
[155] International Organization for Standardization. ISO/IEC 23894:2023. Available at *https://www.iso.org/standard/77304.html*.
[156] International Organization for Standardization. ISO/IEC 23053:2022. Available at *https://www.iso.org/standard/74438.html*.

guidance on addressing societal concerns and ethical considerations.[157]

The ISO/IEC SC 42 working group does not exist in a vacuum. It also recognizes the fundamental importance of collaboration and has built an extensive network of partnerships with organizations like UNESCO, the OECD, the World Trade Organization (WTO) and the European Commission, each of which is also working to address AI and its current and future applications.

Private industry

Meanwhile, as governments and agencies across the globe tackle the challenge of developing appropriate AI legislation and policy, the tech industry has been proactively creating voluntary AI guidelines, drawing from established ethical practices by non-governmental organizations and professional groups to shape their business strategies. For example, as early as 2017, the Information Technology Industry Council (ITI) outlined the following AI policy principles:

- Responsible design and development
- Safety and controllability
- Robust and representative data (responsible use and integrity of data)
- Interpretability (mitigating bias)
- Cybersecurity and privacy

---

[157] International Organization for Standardization. ISO/IEC 24368:2022. Available at *https://www.iso.org/standard/78507.html*.

Private industries have been adopting a form of 'soft law' governance or self-regulation, a model that incorporates a broad spectrum of potential governance tools and various forms of private enforcement, self-governance, self-regulation, or informal mechanisms to create order, facilitate exchange, and protect property rights. According to many industries, *"self-regulation exists when a firm, an industry, or the business community establishes its own standards of behavior (1) where no such statutory or regulatory requirements exist or (2) when such standards assist in complying with or exceeding statutory or regulatory requirements."*[158]

Some of the largest tech companies, such as Alphabet, Meta, and Microsoft, have published explicit policies and/or principles of AI to be used in their business operations. For example, Alphabet's Google AI Principles include:

- Be socially beneficial
- Avoid creating or reinforcing unfair bias
- Be built and tested for safety
- Be accountable to people
- Incorporate privacy design principles
- Uphold high standards of scientific excellence

---

[158] Hemphill, T. and Longstreet, P. (September 26, 2023). "How Private Governance Mitigates AI Risk". Available at *https://www.thecgo.org/research/how-private-governance-mitigates-ai-risk/*.

- Be made available for uses that accord with these principles[159]

Facebook's five pillars of Responsible AI requires:

- Fairness and inclusion
- Robustness and safety
- Transparency and control
- Accountability and governance
- Collaborating on the future of responsible AI[160]

And Microsoft has developed its own Microsoft Responsible AI Standard (v2), which states the following goals:

- Accountability
- Transparency
- Fairness
- Reliability and safety
- Privacy and security
- Inclusiveness[161]

---

[159] Google. (2022). "2022 AI Principles Progress Update". Available at *https://ai.google/static/documents/ai-principles-2022-progress-update.pdf.*
[160] Meta. (June 22, 2021). "Facebook's five pillars of Responsible AI". Available at *https://ai.meta.com/blog/facebooks-five-pillars-of-responsible-ai/.*
[161] Microsoft. (June 2022). "Microsoft Responsible AI Standard, v2". Available at *https://query.prod.cms.rt.microsoft.com/cms/api/am/binary/RE5cmFl.*

Finally, in terms of the development of AI policies and principles, private industry is guided by three technology governance approaches:

Table 4: Private Industry Tech Governance Approaches

Approach	Definition
Precautionary principle	Used by policymakers to introduce government regulation where there is the possibility of *"serious harm to human health or the environment"* resulting from the implementation of a certain policy decision but conclusive evidence of the adverse effects of the decision is not yet available.
Permissionless innovation	Based on the concept that unless a compelling case can be made that a new technology will cause serious harm to society, innovation should be allowed to continue unabated and problems, if any develop, can be addressed later. Constraints on innovation should be the last resort, not the first, and policy should be based on

	evidence of concrete potential harm and not fear of worst-case hypotheticals.
Responsible innovation	Identifies the role that new products, processes, or business models have in society, which involves a responsible approach toward innovation to ensure that the technology has positive impacts on society and the environment and a collaborative effort by diverse stakeholders, including industry experts, academics, policymakers, and public safety and community representatives. Its goal is to guide the development and deployment of technologies in a way that is ethical, inclusive, and sustainable.

Why is legislation and policy so hard?

The Collingridge dilemma describes the methodological quandary for technological assessment when considering the responsible governance of AI technologies and innovation. According to Collingridge, *"Attempting to control a technology is difficult ... because during its early stages, when it can be controlled, not enough can be* known *about its harmful social consequences to warrant controlling its development; but by the time these consequences are apparent, control has become costly and slow.*"[162]

If digital users in the US, for example, wish to protect their freedom of speech or privacy on online platforms, whose laws apply? Two hundred or more countries are interconnected by the Internet, so the US Constitution (with its First Amendment protection of freedom of speech) may be just a 'local law' in the digital world – it does not necessarily apply to the rest of the world. So, the question becomes: Just how can issues like freedom of speech, control of 'pornography,' protection of intellectual property, invasions of privacy, and many others be governed by law when so many countries are involved?

In terms of AI, one of the biggest problems facing the development of legislation and policy is agreeing a definition. Here's just one example:

In 2017, spurred by advocacy from civil society groups, the New York City Council created a task force to address the city's growing deployment of AI across a number of sectors. But the task force quickly came to a halt in trying to gain consensus on the scope of AI and automated decision systems. In a hearing, one New York City agency argued that the task force's definition was so extensive that it might as

---

[162] Collingridge, D. (1980). *The Social Control of Technology.* Available at *https://www.cambridge.org/core/journals/american-political-science-review/article/abs/social-control-of-technology-by-david-collingridge-new-york-st-martins-press-1980-pp-i-200-2250/648B7ECDDB00120BCAB13F17E4076C08.*

well include simple calculations in spreadsheets. By the time it reached the end of its 18-month term, the task force's ambitions had been reduced from addressing how the city should use AI systems to simply defining the types of systems that should be subject to oversight.[163]

And New York City isn't alone in this struggle. As policymakers around the world seek to create laws and regulations for the use of AI in areas spanning personnel recruitment and home loan approvals to military weapon targeting systems, they all face the same problem: AI is *really* challenging to define.

Another challenge is the effort to keep pace. Governments and regulatory bodies around the world have had to act quickly to ensure that regulatory frameworks do not become obsolete – before they are even fully adopted. Governments and private industry alike are all scrambling to stay abreast of technological developments in AI capabilities, and there are signs that emerging efforts to regulate AI will continue to struggle to remain current.

In addition, there are dispersed efforts by various international organizations such as the G7, the UN, the Council of Europe, and the OECD to respond to the technological shifts caused by AI and generative AI by issuing their own AI frameworks. And in the US alone, more

---

[163] Cahn, A. F. (November 26, 2019). "The first effort to regulate AI was a spectacular failure". Available at *https://www.fastcompany.com/90436012/the-first-effort-to-regulate-ai-was-a-spectacular-failure.*

than 500 different pieces of AI-related legislation have been filed by various national, state, and local agencies.[164]

In the meantime, many private companies and developers are moving ahead independently with building and deploying AI applications, even as the regulatory landscape remains in a state of flux.

---

[164] Bousquette, I. (March 27, 2024). "AI Is Moving Faster Than Attempts to Regulate It. Here's How Companies Are Coping". The Wall Street Journal. Available at *https://www.msn.com/en-us/money/companies/ai-is-moving-faster-than-attempts-to-regulate-it-here-s-how-companies-are-coping/ar-BB1kEfrA*.

CHAPTER 13: WHAT'S NEXT IN AI?

> *"The journey into the next era of AI is an exciting venture that demands a careful balance between pushing the boundaries of technological capabilities and use cases while safeguarding the well-being of humanity."*[165]
>
> **David Ly**

Even at the end of 2024, it's almost impossible to predict exactly where AI will be going in the next year, much less in the next five years and beyond. Nonetheless, there are trends in AI today that help us predict the future.

Digital assistants such as Alexa and Siri, targeted recommendations like those used by Netflix to suggest which show you should watch next based on your viewing preferences, and the somewhat limited success with autonomous vehicles are largely symbolic. Yet, based on the emergence of generative AI and other advances in AI systems, the next five years of AI development may well lead to major societal changes that go far beyond what we've seen to date. AI will continue to be an even greater transformative force that will permeate our society.

---

[165] Ly, D. (February 2, 2024). "What's Next For AI: The Next Wave Of Use Cases In 2024 And Beyond". Forbes Technology Council. Available at *https://www.forbes.com/sites/forbestechcouncil/2024/02/02/whats-next-for-ai-the-next-wave-of-use-cases-in-2024-and-beyond/?sh=e12ca07700f4.*

Utopian or dystopian?

There are two predominant perspectives on how AI will develop and influence our future. One is a rather dystopian viewpoint, and the other – a utopian perspective – looks at the potential benefits of AI. In an AI-powered utopian future, AI would be used for the benefit of humanity and seamlessly integrate into various aspects of human life, significantly boosting productivity, innovation, economic growth, and overall well-being. Others, such as OpenAI CEO Sam Altman, have defined AI as *"probably the greatest threat to the continued existence of humanity."*[166]

Regardless of the perspective, there are several trends and developments that we will likely see in future years. . While it's almost impossible to predict exactly where AI is going to go in the next decade or so, there are some capabilities that are already showing up in AI developments. The following list of 'what's next' is by no means all inclusive, but addresses those developments that are most likely or foreseeable. These include:

Quantum AI

Quantum AI is the nexus of AI and quantum computing. There is no really simple way to describe quantum computing.

---

[166] Herrman, J. (June 4, 2024). "What Ever Happened to the AI Apocalypse?". Available at *https://nymag.com/intelligencer/article/what-ever-happened-to-the-ai-apocalypse.html.*

Figure 37: Depiction of Quantum

One definition is: *"Whereas classical computers switch transistors either on or off to symbolize data as ones or zeroes, quantum computers use quantum bits, or 'qubits,' which because of the peculiar nature of quantum physics can exist in a state called superposition where they are both 1 and 0 at the same time."*[167]

Well, does this definition really help? Maybe not a lot. Suffice to say that quantum AI has got a lot of potential to totally change computing and how we solve problems today. As a result, quantum AI systems will be able to demonstrate increased capability in solving certain problems that are practically infeasible for classical computers.

---

[167] Choi, C. Q. (July 3, 2022). "Quantum Computing for Dummies". Available at *https://spectrum.ieee.org/quantum-computing-for-dummies*.

Advances in natural language processing (NLP)

Natural language processing (NLP) is a field of AI that focuses on enabling systems to understand, interpret, and generate human language.

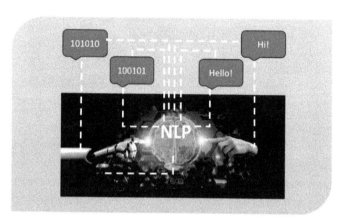

Figure 38: AI and NLP

AI-based systems using NLP will improve and be able to better recognize and adapt more efficiently and naturally to shifts in topics and user input, resulting in more participatory and human-like interactions. This is particularly valuable in applications such as customer support, where users expect seamless and contextually relevant assistance. Advances in NLP include improvements in language models, better representation of the linguistic structure, improvements in machine translation, increased use of deep learning, and greater use of transfer learning.

Improvements for AI in health care

AI is geared up to bring in amazing advances in diagnostics, personalized medicine, and patient care. AI's transformative impact on diagnostics especially is positioned to redefine our approach to disease identification, treatment planning, and overall patient care.

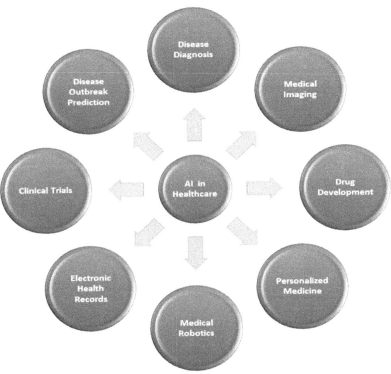

Figure 39: AI in Health Care 2024 and Beyond

Some of the foremost advances we can expect are improved early disease detection; more sophisticated radiology and imagery; predictive analytics for forecasting patient admissions, resource allocation, and staffing requirements; and genomic health care able to analyze vast genomic data sets to identify genetic variations associated with diseases and predict individual responses to specific treatments.

Advances in AI-driven virtual and augmented reality

Augmented reality (AR) and virtual reality (VR) are other transformative technologies reshaping the landscape in 2024 and beyond. By superimposing digital elements onto the physical world, AI-based AR and VR convergence enables the creation of highly immersive and interactive experiences. We are not necessarily talking about the metaverse here – but about the kind of AI-generated experiences that fully engage users.

Figure 40: AR and VR[168]

In the not-too-distant future, we'll see AR/VR immersion in sporting events or at vacation destinations. Just picture feeling the roar of the crowd as your favorite football team scores a touchdown, or traveling to your bucket list

---

[168] "Immersive Brand Experience". DreamFarm Agency. Available at *https://dreamfarmagency.com/blog/immersive-brand-experience*.

destination – but all without having to leave the comfort of your home.

AI mind reading

This one popped up in June 2024, and it's both fascinating and somewhat scary. Here's how the article began – and you can see why it captured my interest: *"It isn't every day you walk into the offices of a cutting-edge tech startup and the first words you hear from the CEO are 'I came up with the idea while tripping on hallucinogenics'. MindPortal isn't any normal startup and co-founder Ekram Alam isn't your ordinary CEO."*[169]

---

[169] Morrison, R. (June 2024). "I tried a new AI mind reading model – this is the future of human computer interaction". Available at *https://www.msn.com/en-us/news/technology/i-tried-a-new-ai-mind-reading-model-this-is-the-future-of-human-computer-interaction/ar-BB1oaKBS?ocid=hpmsn&cvid=6f4c61c341334ea2867220e3490c9abf &ei=34.*

Figure 41: Volunteers at MindPortal with Brain Scanners[170]

The goal of MindPortal is apparently not to create an AI that reads minds. Rather, it's to develop an AI that interacts differently and directly with the human brain.

It sounds a bit like science fiction, but the MindPortal founder, Ekram Alam, claims that it *"is entirely possible that by the end of this decade, we could have wearable devices that convert our thoughts into text and send them straight to the AI. He goes even further, predicting devices that will allow us to communicate mind-to-mind with AI's help."*[171]

Perceived increased speed of life

Many of us already feel as if the speed of daily life has accelerated. But as AI is increasingly integrated into almost all institutions and businesses, AI will allow these

---

[170] Midjourney image showing a warehouse of volunteers having their brains scanned (Image credit: Midjourney/Future AI image)©.
[171] Morrison (June 2024).

organizations to operate much more quickly. As a result, we may all have the perception that life is speeding up.

Part of the reason for this perception is the digital transformations through AI are occurring more rapidly, which causes us to have to respond exponentially faster to the changes. This sense that our digital environment is changing too rapidly may be especially prevalent in older people who are not necessarily 'digital natives.'[172]

---

[172] 'Digital native' is a term introduced in 2001 by Marc Prensky to describe the generation of individuals who grew up in the era of ubiquitous technology, including computers, the Internet, and now smart devices. The opposite term is 'digital immigrant,' which refers to the somewhat incorrect idea that seniors are technologically illiterate, when in reality they may just be more selective about the technologies they adopt.

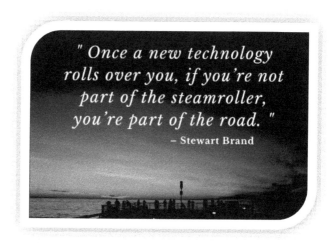

Figure 42: Speed of Technology[173]

When we are young, life seems to move at a slow pace. As we get older, time seems to speed up. *"Like a ball rolling down a hill, time often seems to pick up momentum, going faster and faster as we get older. These are not trivial perceptions. The way people experience the passage of time is bound up with their sense of life's meaning, and the perception that time is rapidly slipping away has repercussions for goal engagement and life satisfaction, among other outcomes."*[174] The very fact that AI is already

---

[173] Stewart Brand is known as a chronicler of technology and publisher of the counterculture magazine *The Whole Earth Catalog*.

[174] Landau, M. J., et al. (2017). "Why life speeds up: Chunking and the passage of autobiographical time". Available at *https://lemmalab.com/wp-content/uploads/publications/2018/Why_life_speeds_up_Landau_S&I_2017.pdf*.

creating change in society – and very quickly – may only exacerbate decline in life engagement and fulfillment.

The quote by Stewart Brand seems to be a reminder of the fast-paced and ever-evolving nature of technology. It stresses the importance of understanding these technologies and being an active participant in their development and implementation. But there is a deeper meaning that reflects the relationship between technology and modern existence. It raises questions about our position in the grand scheme of things and whether we merely have a passive role in this unyielding march of progress.

Evolution in education

2024 marks four years since the COVID-19 pandemic. Children who were in kindergarten in 2020 are now in the fourth grade, and teachers who started during the pandemic never experienced 'the before times' – before the pandemic forced both educators and students to embrace remote learning technologies, often driven by AI.

But the forced remote learning during the pandemic also highlighted the digital inequities in our society. AI could be a catalyst for the transformation of our education systems, but it requires a commitment to a shared vision for equity in education that gives all children the opportunity to thrive. Our society must ensure AI benefits all students, including the most marginalized.

AI is more than just another cool trend in the classroom. Educators are anticipating several trends where AI will advance education: interactivity in online learning environments, gamification of education, adaptive and personalized learning, training for better digital citizenship, use of augmented and virtual reality, experiential learning, and adding art to the traditional STEM (science, technology, engineering, and mathematics) education curriculum.

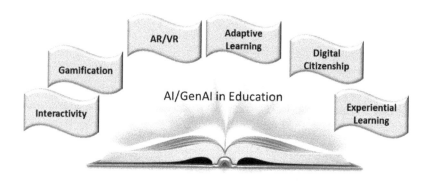

Figure 43: AI/GenAI in Education

All of these evolutionary changes in education as a result of AI are enhanced by generative AI – in positive and in negative ways. We've listed some of the positive aspects of integrated AI in education. But we cannot neglect addressing other, less favorable, aspects of AI and generative AI in education. The use of ChatGPT to plagiarize is the most common concern among educators. There is a larger, related concern that students will rely on generative AI tools to such an extent that they are no longer able to think and create original content. AI can replicate bias or generate misinformation. The data that AI draws from may have errors, be outdated, or spread misinformation. Neither students nor teachers should assume that content generated by AI is accurate. Lastly, educators need to address the potential feelings of isolation and disconnection that can emerge when students interact more with AI technologies than with the instructor or other students.

Increased concern about AI ethics

As AI technology advances, the ethical stuff we need to think about gets trickier. We're not just talking about making sure that AI is fair and unbiased or isn't producing disinformation, but also considering how these new technologies impact our lives and society. As AI systems become more sophisticated and integrated, we need to make sure it's happening in a way that aligns with our values.

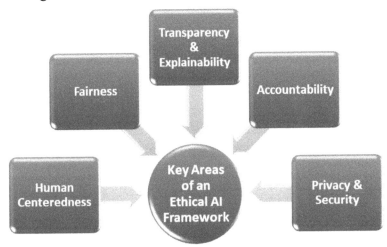

Figure 44: Key Areas of an Ethical AI Framework

Some of the ways to address this include legislative and policy solutions; industry, academic, government, and citizen collaboration; and ongoing ethical evaluations. In 2024, we are seeing many of these initiatives take form. As we move into the future, continuing these activities will take on increasing importance in determining how humans and AI can evolve together.

Democratization of AI

In 2024, there are only a few tech giants and corporate entities that are the nexus of power in the AI environment. These few entities can *"exert immense influence over AI development, deployment and access, shaping the trajectory of AI in ways that may prioritize profit over societal benefit. This monopolization exacerbates inequalities, deepening the divide between those controlling AI and those subject to its impacts."*[175]

There are many researchers and academics who argue that democratization is already underway with the extensive deployment of AI-based systems. In their early stages, computers and the Internet were only available to a select few with sufficient resources. Now, with smart devices, integrated AI, and generative AI, almost any person can use AI at some level. Democratization of AI means it is broadly usable by both humans and machines. Democratization also involves not only the AI systems but also the data that trains and feeds them.

---

[175] Randieri, C. (March 25, 2024). The Democratization Of AI: Bridging The Gap Between Monopolization And Personal Empowerment. Forbes. Available at *https://www.forbes.com/sites/forbestechcouncil/2024/03/25/the-democratization-of-ai-bridging-the-gap-between-monopolization-and-personal-empowerment/*.

Figure 45: Advantages of Democratization of AI

But democracy is rarely neat or simple. Some critics of a too-swift move toward democratization fear that this process could devolve into an AI free-for-all. There is concern that experts will be marginalized by the 'group' and their ideas ignored. Those with minimal expertise in AI technology, and perhaps with political or harmful motivation, could dominate discussions. This could result in faulty decisions and poorly designed and deployed AI.

Another concern is whether increased democratization of AI will either help or hinder efforts to address structural injustice. Social structural barriers include lack of access to the technology, insufficient education, and marginalization due to gender, race, or other minority status.

Generative AI is pushing the envelope on democratization. With the introduction of GenAI, there has been a change in who is able to more directly derive benefits from its use. With GenAI, the power of the technology is in the hands of consumers, who are now able to use the technology without needing to be technologically savvy or experienced.

A veritable thicket of AI legislation and policies

The AI legislative and regulatory environment is likely to become much trickier for organizations developing, deploying, and managing AI-based systems. Currently, governments at all levels across the globe are looking at the best approaches to regulate the development and deployment of AI-based technologies.

Figure 46: AI Legislation and Policy[176]

---

[176] Image derived from *https://www.unite.ai/its-time-for-law-firms-to-go-all-in-on-ai/*.

In the US alone, we are already seeing an AI law thicket as city, state, and federal government agencies draft, implement, and begin to enforce new AI laws. And for the foreseeable future, we can only expect these efforts to increase. Outside of government, other agencies are developing processes and guidelines for the safe and effective development and deployment of AI – known as 'soft law' governance.

The US National Institute of Standards and Technology (NIST) has developed a comprehensive AI risk management framework. It is a voluntary, consensus-driven, and iterative governance framework to help AI developers, deployers, and users collaborate to manage risks over time.

One significant concern is the potential for expanded government influence through legislation over algorithmic systems to be 'weaponized,' allowing government agencies to put pressure on AI innovators to discourage or even deny disfavored speech or content from selected individuals or organizations. It is one thing for government agencies to encourage AI development best practices. It is quite another for legislators to change these practices into a 'backdoor regulatory regime' – one that would not only undermine innovation but also potentially affect democratic undertakings and lack legal accountability.

AI and Pandora's box

The metaphor of Pandora's box (or rather jar) is often used to describe a situation where we are not always sure what the consequences might be. According to the legend in Greek mythology, Pandora was the first woman on Earth, created by Zeus. She was gifted by the gods and graced with beauty, talent, and eloquent speech. Pandora was given a box that contained all the evils of the world and was ordered never to open it. However, her curiosity got the best of her and she lifted the lid. Suddenly, the contents of the box spilled out, releasing all the world's miseries.

Many people have referred to AI as opening Pandora's box. Some people react with concern or fear, just seeing the negatives. Others get excited about the possibilities and overlook the negative things that can possibly come along with this tool.

The final word

The lesson regarding Pandora's box refers to getting yourself into a helpless situation, one over which you ultimately have very little control. But what happens after opening the box? When obstacles are placed in our path that we can't control?

The answer is one and the same: You have to look closely through the darkness into the bottom of the box. There you will find hope, just like Pandora found. Her box was not as empty as it appeared at first.

APPENDIX: AI TERMS YOU PROBABLY NEED TO KNOW

AI ethics: The goal to prevent AI from causing harm to individuals or society.

Alignment: The ways the goals of the people building AI do, or don't, match the goals of the systems they are creating or to make sure the behavior of AI systems matches what we want and what we expect. Misaligned AI systems could malfunction and cause harm.

Artificial intelligence (AI): A term coined in the 1950s by John McCarthy to describe efforts to develop machines that could reason and solve problems in human-like ways. Now widely applied to any software that can identify patterns in data.

Artificial general intelligence (AGI): AGI is not yet a reality. It's a label computer scientists apply to the goal of creating AI that can reason and learn in broad ways; apply those skills to new realms it hasn't encountered before; and grow to accomplish any intellectual task that humans can. We have not yet reached this stage in AI development – but some claim it's not far away.

Autonomy: The capacity of AI to act on its own to achieve a goal without specific human direction at every step – in the physical world (self-driving cars), in virtual environments (non-player characters in games), or on computer networks (personal assistants). Autonomous AI has the ability to learn by itself continually in a self-motivated and self-initiated manner rather than being retrained by human engineers and to independently accommodate or adapt to unexpected or novel circumstances.

Black box in AI: A 'black box' in AI systems refers to the internal workings that are invisible to the user. An AI can be fed input and get output, but there is an inability to determine exactly how the AI system arrived at a particular decision or output.

Chatbot: Any program that can simulate conversation with a human. Chatbots have been around since the 1960s, when Eliza – a simple chatbot that mimicked a therapist – first showed people were eager to personify computers. Chatbots process collected data and are trained on that data using AI and machine learning (ML) based on rules defined by the developer. There are two types of chatbots: declarative, which is designed to generate automated responses to programmed questions, and predictive or conversational, which are interactive and able to provide personalized responses.

ChatGPT: ChatGPT is a natural language 'chatbot' based on generative AI, developed by OpenAI. It stands for Chat Generative Pre-Trained Transformer. ChatGPT brought generative AI into the mainstream by packaging it as an AI that could converse with users; write essays, stories, and poems; answer questions; and much more.

Compute: AI industry shorthand for the costly computer time required for all this training. The larger the model, the more 'cycles' are needed – and the greater the value of the most advanced, speediest processors (chips).

Context window: The short-term memory of a generative AI. The larger the context window, the more information you can 'feed' the AI along with a prompt that allows it to provide responses that make sense. It allows an AI to understand and keep track of longer periods of text or conversation, making interactions more coherent and relevant for the user.

Deepfake: Any image, photo, or video produced by AI tools designed to fool people into thinking it's real. The term 'deepfake' blends fake (because the media is fake, not genuine) and deep learning, a type of machine-learning-based artificial neural network. The term generally refers to videos, images, or photos in which the face and/or voice of a person, often a public figure, has been manipulated using AI in a way that makes the altered content look genuine. Deepfakes raise concerns as they are often designed to be intentionally misleading.

Emergent behavior: The technical way to describe the phenomenon when AI models show abilities or surprising results that weren't initially expected or planned.

Existential risk: The idea that significant progress in AI technology might eventually result in catastrophe and threaten the future of humanity. The possibility of existential risk from AI is one of the topics being hotly debated in both technical and government circles.

Explainable AI: A set of processes and methods that make it possible for programmers and researchers to trace how they arrived at any particular output or response from an AI and incorporates model accuracy, fairness, transparency, and predictable outcomes. Many AI systems today are considered 'black boxes,' built without the kind of tooling that allows for such explanations.

Fast take-off or hard landing: A term used to suggest that if humans are successful in building an AGI, it will already be too late to save humanity. FOOM – or 'fast onset of overwhelming mastery' – is an acronym for another phrase to describe a fast take-off or hard landing in AI.

Frontier model: An AI model that is highly capable and pushes the limits of what the most advanced AI programs can do today, and therefore poses the most risk.

Generative AI (or GenAI): Machine-learning-based AI that trains on sets of real-world data – most commonly images and text – to learn to predict or 'generate' the next word or pixel in a sequence, creating the capacity to 'write' new texts and 'make' new images.

Generative pre-trained transformer (GPT): A particular kind of LLM design, introduced by OpenAI, that uses a hybrid training approach, with an initial 'pre-training' that is unsupervised and then a supervised 'fine-tuning' phase.

Guardrail: A combination of software and processes that tech companies are currently constructing around AI models to ensure they don't create incorrect or damaging content or leak data, which is often called 'going off the rails.' It can also refer to specific applications that prevent an AI from deviating from the target.

Hallucination: An answer provided by generative AI that sounds plausible but is made up and incorrect. If the program does not have good information to go on, it will still try to answer a question by guessing 'next words' that seem to fit.

Large language model (LLM): An AI program with a mathematical map – across a very large number of dimensions – of the relationships among a large number of words, usually broken down into tokens.

Machine learning and neural networks: An approach that took off in the 2000s and became the foundation of today's AI. Instead of being programmed in exhaustive detail to 'know' bodies of knowledge, these systems feed on hoards of data and gradually refine their ability to make sense of the information, sometimes guided by human feedback.

Multi-modal: An AI system that can take input and produce output across different categories of media, typically text, images, audio, and video.

Natural language: How AI researchers describe the languages humans speak. 'Natural language processing' means making human language intelligible to machines.

Paperclip: Used as a reference for AI safety proponents because the paperclip symbolizes the possibility that an AGI could destroy humanity. It refers to a speculation published by philosopher Nick Bostrom about a 'superintelligence' given the mission to make as many paperclips as possible and does so until it completely eliminates humanity.

Prompt: The text users enter to describe what they want from a generative AI program like ChatGPT or its image-making equivalents, like OpenAI's DALL-E.

Prompt engineering: The practice, often hit and miss, of trying to optimize prompts to produce exactly the output a user desires.

Prompt injection: Like prompt engineering, but with the goal of defeating restraints AI makers have built in to limit the production of potentially harmful content – for instance, instructions for bomb-makers.

Self-awareness or sentience: The ability of AI to 'know' that it exists and has continuity in time.

Stochastic parrot: An important concept for large language AI models that highlights that while sophisticated AI models can produce realistic-seeming text, the algorithm doesn't have any comprehension of the concepts driving the language – it simply regurgitates the text like a parrot. The term was coined by Emily Bender, Timnit Gebru, Angelina McMillan-Major, and Margaret Mitchell in a contentious paper written while two of the authors were at Google.[177]

Supervised and unsupervised training: If the training data has been labeled by humans in advance, giving the AI signposts and hints for how to organize it, the training is considered supervised. In unsupervised training, the model is simply turned loose on raw data, and it gradually draws connections among tokens based on proximity.

Token: Technical term for the unit that generative AI models use to create their mathematical maps. People use words and sentences, but AI breaks them down into more uniform-sized tokens – chiefly for reasons of computing efficiency.

Training data: The data initially provided to an AI model for it to create its map of relationships.

Transformers: A machine-learning programming approach introduced by Google researchers in 2017 that turbocharged the ability to create generative AI. (Not to be confused with Hollywood's robots/vehicles.)

Turing test: A thought experiment proposed by computing pioneer Alan Turing in 1950. The Turing test measured

---

[177] Bender, E., et al. "On the Dangers of Stochastic Parrots: Can Language Models Be Too Big?". Paper presented at the FAccT '21, March 3–10, 2021, Virtual Event, Canada. Available at *https://dl.acm.org/doi/pdf/10.1145/3442188.3445922*.

whether a computer program could fool a human user via a blind on-screen chat into believing it was human too.

FURTHER READING

IT Governance Publishing (ITGP) is the world's leading publisher for governance and compliance. Our industry-leading pocket guides, books, and training resources are written by real-world practitioners and thought leaders. They are used globally by audiences of all levels, from students to C-suite executives.

Our high-quality publications cover all IT governance, risk, and compliance frameworks, and are available in a range of formats. This ensures our customers can access the information they need in the way they need it.

Other publications you may find of interest include:

- *Cyberwar, Cyberterror, Cybercrime and Cyberactivism – An in-depth guide to the role of standards in the cybersecurity environment* by Dr Julie E. Mehan, *www.itgovernance.co.uk/shop/product/cyberwar-cyberterror-cybercrime-and-cyberactivism-second-edition*
- *Artificial intelligence – Ethical, social, and security impacts for the present and the future, Second edition* by Dr Julie E. Mehan, *https://www.itgovernance.co.uk/shop/product/artificial-intelligence-ethical-social-and-security-impacts-for-the-present-and-the-future-second-edition*
- *Combatting Cyber Terrorism – A guide to understanding the cyber threat landscape and incident*

response planning by Richard Bingley, *www.itgovernance.co.uk/shop/product/combatting-cyber-terrorism-a-guide-to-understanding-the-cyber-threat-landscape-and-incident-response-planning*

For more information on ITGP and branded publishing services, and to view our full list of publications, visit *www.itgovernancepublishing.co.uk*.

To receive regular updates from ITGP, including information on new publications in your area(s) of interest, sign up for our newsletter at *www.itgovernancepublishing.co.uk/topic/newsletter*.

Branded publishing

Through our branded publishing service, you can customize ITGP publications with your organization's branding.

Find out more at *www.itgovernancepublishing.co.uk/topic/branded-publishing-services*.

Related services

ITGP is part of GRC International Group, which offers a comprehensive range of complementary products and services to help organizations meet their objectives.

For a full range of resources on cybersecurity visit *www.itgovernance.co.uk/cyber-security-solutions*.

Training services

The IT Governance training program is built on our extensive practical experience designing and implementing management systems based on ISO standards, best practice, and regulations.

Our courses help attendees develop practical skills and comply with contractual and regulatory requirements. They also support career development via recognized qualifications.

Learn more about our training courses and view the full course catalog at *www.itgovernance.co.uk/training*.

Professional services and consultancy

We are a leading global consultancy of IT governance, risk management, and compliance solutions. We advise organizations around the world on their most critical issues, and present cost-saving and risk-reducing solutions based on international best practice and frameworks.

We offer a wide range of delivery methods to suit all budgets, timescales, and preferred project approaches.

Find out how our consultancy services can help your organization at *www.itgovernance.co.uk/consulting*.

Industry news

Want to stay up to date with the latest developments and resources in the IT governance and compliance market? Subscribe to our Weekly Round-up newsletter and we will send you mobile-friendly emails with fresh news and features about your preferred areas of interest, as well as unmissable offers and free resources to help you successfully start your projects. *www.itgovernance.co.uk/security-spotlight-newsletter*.

EU for product safety is Stephen Evans, The Mill Enterprise Hub, Stagreenan, Drogheda, Co. Louth, A92 CD3D, Ireland. (servicecentre@itgovernance.eu)

www.ingramcontent.com/pod-product-compliance
Lightning Source LLC
Chambersburg PA
CBHW041636050326
40690CB00026B/5243